MONROVIA MODERN

Monrovia Modern
Urban Form and Political Imagination in Liberia

Danny Hoffman

Duke University Press   Durham and London   2017

© 2017 Duke University Press
All rights reserved
Printed in Korea on acid-free paper ∞
Designed by Heather Hensley
Typeset in Minion Pro by Copperline

Cataloging-in-Publication Data is available from
the Library of Congress.

ISBN 978-0-8223-6357-6 (hardcover : alk. paper)
ISBN 978-0-8223-5884-8 (pbk. : alk. paper)
ISBN 978-0-8223-7308-7 (ebook)

Cover art: E. J. Roye. Photo by Danny Hoffman.

Duke University Press gratefully acknowledges the support of
the University of Washington, Department of Anthropology,
which provided funds toward the production of this book.

Porte cochère, Liberia Broadcasting System

Dedicated, as all things are, to
Julie, Corey Rose, Lucy, and Eve.

Modern architecture, and its extension
into town planning, has above all this
task . . . of making industrialism fit
for human use; [making] buildings and
larger aggregations in which life may
know its bounds and flourish.
—Maxwell Fry and Jane Drew,
architects and advisors to the
British colonies in West Africa, 1956

haha → colonialists
what dicks

Contents

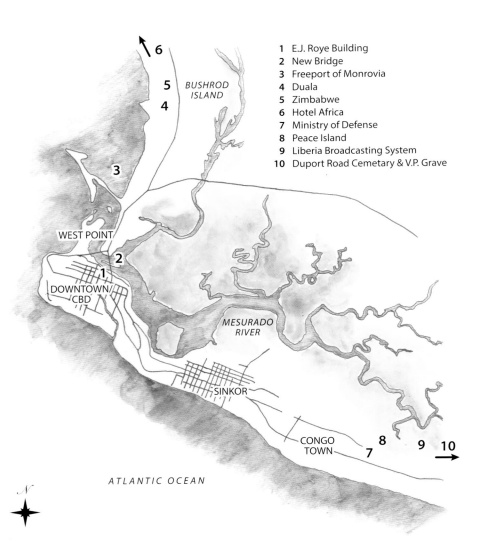

6
5
4
BUSHROD
ISLAND

1   E.J. Roye Building
2   New Bridge
3   Freeport of Monrovia
4   Duala
5   Zimbabwe
6   Hotel Africa
7   Ministry of Defense
8   Peace Island
9   Liberia Broadcasting System
10 Duport Road Cemetary & V.P. Grave

3

WEST POINT

2
1
DOWNTOWN/
CBD

MESURADO
RIVER

SINKOR

CONGO
TOWN   8   9   10
       7

ATLANTIC OCEAN

N

Illustrations

This is a story told largely through four buildings as they existed in early 2012. Each was a landmark in Monrovia, the capital of Liberia. When the long decade of fighting ended in this part of West Africa in 2003, all four lay in ruins.

The oldest, the E. J. Roye Building, was for many years the most prominent built form in the city. From the early 1960s it was the headquarters of the True Whig Party, a high modernist testament to Liberia's history of one-party rule. During the 2003 siege of Monrovia, the forces of then president Charles Taylor posted gunmen throughout the building's eight floors. From there they sought to prevent rebel forces from crossing the bridge into the city center.

Two of the buildings were brutalist constructions, massive concrete edifices intended to house government ministries and services. The Ministry of Defense and the Liberia Broadcasting System were both commissioned in the 1980s by Samuel Doe, the young military commander whose presidency ended 133 years of rule by the nation's Americo-Liberian minority. During and after the war both buildings were home to hundreds of refugees, internally displaced people, and ex-combatants from the various fighting factions.

The final structure is a five-star hotel, the Hotel Africa. Its remains sit on a beach at the outskirts of the city. Liberian elites, expatriate relief and development workers, and a cosmopolitan class of financiers and traffickers once swam in the hotel's Africa-shaped pool and gambled in its large casino. As rebel forces advanced on the capital in the final clashes of the Mano River war,

deconstruction

the residents of a slum settlement next to the hotel quickly took the building apart as they scavenged useful or saleable materials.

In their design and construction, each of these four structures represents a vision of the modern city and the modern African state. So, too, do their ruins. These are visions that map uneasily onto one another and onto the struggles many Monrovians face as they shape a future for themselves in this "aftermodern" city (Enwezor 2010). These mismatches and mismappings are the subject of the book. *these*

Because this is a story told through built forms, *Monrovia Modern* is a book about architecture. But it is a book about architecture viewed through the prism of my own long thinking about violence in contemporary West Africa. As an anthropologist focused on this region's recent conflicts and their aftermath, my approach to the built environment is rooted in a concern with how young people in Monrovia, particularly young ex-combatant men, inhabit the material world around them.

Architecture has long been an issue of importance to anthropologists, but an emerging literature of materialisms has reinvigorated the theoretical and ethnographic possibilities for thinking the built environment anthropologically. Works by Victor Buchli (2013), Tim Ingold (2013), and Mélanie van door Horn (2009) exemplify attempts to theorize the materiality of architecture as an anthropological problem. A good many more texts have taken complex organic and inorganic assemblages as their object of study, assemblages that include the built environment. Ethnographies by Alex Nading (2014), Kristin Peterson (2014), and Mun Young Cho (2013) are not about architecture or built form per se. But they incorporate sophisticated analysis of the structural forms of the city into projects that remain resolutely devoted to the anthropological project of understanding urban "lifeworlds" (Jackson 2012).

While *Monrovia Modern* bears a family resemblance to these and other texts that have resulted from critical cultural anthropology's material turn, it is, in the end, very different. It is neither an ethnography of the social life of things nor a metatheorization of architecture as an anthropological object.

What *Monrovia Modern* is, is the story of political imagination and its relationship to the built environment. It is anthropological in its focus on everyday urbanisms in modern Africa. It is anthropological in that it tells the story of how lives are shaped by the city in which they are lived, and how those lives shape the city in turn. But to craft these chapters and their arguments I have relied more heavily on architectural theory than on ethnographic practice.

This is less a thick description than what the landscape historian Thaisa Way (2013) calls a "thick section." Its historical detail and theoretical explorations are not layered onto narrative plotlines, as in Clifford Geertz's (1973) famous definition of ethnography. Instead they are layered upon the architect's drawing, with its concerns for relationships of space, use, form, and representation. The nuances of how humans inhabit those forms is, of course, always the sine qua non of the work. But much of the emphasis and much of the insight is layered on the built forms themselves.

Monrovia Modern follows an earlier book that explored the lives of combatants in the Mano River war, in which Monrovia was one of multiple battlegrounds. *The War Machines* (Hoffman 2011b) analyzed violence as a form of labor for young men in Sierra Leone and Liberia. As the war developed throughout the 1990s and early 2000s, it seemed male youths were increasingly living lives organized through processes of containment, rapid assembly, and deployment. In cities, rural camps, mines, and plantations, young men were propelled by forces larger than themselves through cycles of waiting and movement, cycles determined by the overlapping logics of violence and commerce. The barracks, I argued in *The War Machines*, seemed to have become the organizing principle of West African postmodernity.

The current project extends *The War Machines* both chronologically and theoretically. In the decade since the last open warfare in Monrovia, some of the dynamics of mobility and waiting I described in *The War Machines* have changed. Some elements of the barracks logic have calcified; others have disappeared. The city and what it represents has changed along with new population flows, new streams of capital, and the continued evolution of the global apparatus for the distribution of labor and profit. This project takes up some of those regional and global changes.

In *The War Machines* I argued for a certain conception of space but largely set aside thinking about the materiality of that space. In this project, the question of forms and their habitability comes to the fore. Here I have attempted to understand the built environment of Monrovia not just as the context of unfolding lives, but as part of the machine that produces them. The approach I have taken excavates the "affordances" of forms, to use the literary scholar Caroline Levine's (2015: 5–11) term. It is a mode of inquiry that asks what a given ordering of things, understood as both a material object and as a sociopolitical arrangement, invites and allows us to do.

"What is a walled enclosure or a rhyming couplet *capable* of doing?" Levine writes. "Each shape or pattern, social or literary, lays claim to a limited range of potentialities" (2015: 6). And, by implication, it forecloses others. That is what interests me here.

MONROVIA MODERN RESTS ON three assumptions. The first is that there is no natural or authentic way to live in the urban spaces of the modern world. The material, social, economic, and political activities of creating spaces and occupying them are experimental processes, processes of repeated invention. Urban residents must continuously learn to live an urban existence. In an enigmatic essay that has become a touchstone for architects and architectural theorists, as well as for philosophers and anthropologists of the built environment, Martin Heidegger wrote that "mortals . . . must ever learn to dwell" (1993: 363). Contemporary urban spaces demand constant evolution, a process that is messy and unpredictable. It is also a task at which a city's inhabitants do not always succeed.

My second assumption in this book is that urban warfare lays bare the challenges and opportunities of creating urban lives. The instability and uncertainty of urban ecosystems that have been altered physically, psychically, socially, and economically by widespread violence present occasions for radical experimentation, as well as for virulent forms of reactionary conservatism. Some of the furthest-reaching innovations in politics, philosophy, architecture, and the arts were born from efforts to understand and make city life out of the creative destruction of war.

That said, the urban warscape is not a tabula rasa. Those who live there must wrestle with histories that haunt the city and with powerful forces from within and without that shape its future. They must contend with the city's ruins. *Monrovia Modern* is an effort to understand at least some of those forces, some of the emergent possibilities for living through the ruins of the city's built form and some of the limits those ruins impose.

The final assumption at the heart of this project is that the political and economic flows of the city are sometimes quite distinct. "Urbanization" is originally a term of economy. It describes the techniques for managing a complex marketplace and all of its attendant systems of transportation, communication, and labor. Coined in the 1860s, but with roots going back to Roman imperialism, urbanization names the process through which the ever-

urban = economy
city = political → the production of citizenship

shifting relations of production in the metropolis are regulated and temporarily stabilized.

The city, by contrast, suggests a political ideal. It names a space in which diverse interests meet. It is a site of agonism, the zone for working out the meaning and the mechanics of citizenship and difference. Though these terms, the city and the urban, are often used interchangeably, their orientation and the trajectories they open do not always overlap or intersect.

Indeed, in both social organization and built form it is possible to find urban economic life without citizenship or even political subjectivity. Michel Agier (2002, 2008) vividly describes massive refugee camps like Dadaab in East Africa, camps that have become densely populated urban spaces (meaning they host complex economies and are organized around the functioning of those economies) but are not cities (meaning those who live there have no rights of citizenship or formal political agency). Despite being home to more than 400,000 people,[1] many of whom have now lived there for decades, Dadaab is a space of economic production but not a space for the production of citizens. Its residents live in urban space but politically they belong nowhere.

therefore the urban ≠ city

In an architectural parallel, Pier Vittorio Aureli (2011: 16) describes the contemporary design of many cities as one that produces structures of economic flow but offers no space for political engagement. Much of the modern built environment works to regulate economic relationships. Even radically new kinds of space are often designed purely to accommodate flows of capital and relations of production. More rarely do built forms, or elements within built forms, facilitate the political encounters that transform urban space into political space. There are few contemporary built forms that serve as catalysts or platforms for negotiating collective demands or inventing new kinds of urban citizenship and participation.

Monrovia Modern is an attempt to make particular built forms speak to the nature of urban flows and political imagination—and to do so within the space of possibility of an African city contending with its history of war. My focus is four buildings in a postwar West African capital. But ultimately this is an effort to understand conditions that make it difficult, and sometimes impossible, to learn to dwell.

Acknowledgments

I am grateful to a vast network of family, friends, colleagues, and interlocutors in Liberia, Sierra Leone, France, and the United States. What is successful in this project is the work of many. The errors are my own.

A number of institutions supported *Monrovia Modern* at various points. I am especially grateful to the Andrew W. Mellon Foundation and, at the University of Washington, the Simpson Center for the Humanities, the College of Built Environments, the Robert Bolles and Yasuko Endo Endowment, and the Department of Anthropology. A special thank you to Duke University Press and to Gisela Fosado in particular for their unending patience and support.

Fourth floor, Ministry of Defense. 2012. On the northwest tower,
a Chinese telecommunications firm has installed a cell tower
overlooking the otherwise empty building.

Between 2008 and 2010, hundreds of former fighters with the Government of Liberia Armed Forces and their families were evicted from the Ministry of Defense building in Monrovia. Some had lived in the building for more than a decade. Others arrived in 2005 when they were forced out of the ruins of the Barclay Training Center barracks at the behest of U.S. security contractors. Liberians from all corners of the country were among the building's residents, making for an unusually cosmopolitan and vibrant community.

The hulking ministry was originally one element in a building campaign launched by Samuel Doe, the junior military officer who took over the Liberian presidency following a 1980 coup d'état. Monumental architecture, for Doe as for so many other political leaders, was a project of state making and personal aggrandizement. The ministry building was to be one of the largest structures in West Africa, and one of several government projects that enshrined Doe and his cohort on the Monrovia landscape.

The Ministry of Defense was never finished. War broke out in Liberia at the end of 1989. The Israeli firm contracted to design and construct the building completed its concrete supports but little more. Even before the fighting reached Monrovia, the ministry building was a skeleton, though a structurally sound one. Through successive waves of urban warfare the building became a squatter settlement, a vertical neighborhood of fighting men and their families living rough within the building's raw form. Government soldiers and their dependents from upcountry or from contested neighborhoods in Monrovia were barracked in the structure to defend the man who ultimately succeeded Doe, Liberia's warlord president Charles Taylor. Taylor was ousted in 2003, but the men who fought to defend him remained in the ministry building, squatting in their makeshift community.

Then in 2008 the government of Taylor's successor, Ellen Johnson Sirleaf, ordered the building's occupants to leave. Most moved into the swamps next to the building, attempting to find places for themselves in an already over-crowded slum known as Peace Island. Though they complained bitterly about the eviction, they put up surprisingly little resistance. No one I spoke with in the aftermath of the evictions ever claimed they had a right to stay in the ministry, despite their long residence there.

Major Sandi was an exception. He has lived in the ministry building for ten years. While the building's other residents were evicted, Major Sandi was allowed to remain as caretaker and night watchman. A Chinese telecom company has placed cell towers on the roof of the ministry and so it is useful to have a few eyes on the property. But where once there was a dense, populous community, Major Sandi now lives virtually alone in a closet, surrounded by thousands of square feet of vacant concrete.

Recently the Johnson Sirleaf government has begun a survey of the building. Its original blueprints are gone. No one at the Ministry of Public Works knows exactly how large the building is or how it was configured or constructed. When I asked Major Sandi what he hopes will be done with the building once the survey is complete, he pauses. This, apparently, is not a question he has ever been asked before. "It should be given back to the Ministry of Defense," he says finally. Then: "Maybe a hotel. It would make a nice hotel."

THE QUESTION I PUT to Major Sandi ("What futures can be imagined in ruins like the Ministry of Defense?") and his surreal answer ("It might make a nice hotel") are entry points to a constellation of uncertainties that define many Monrovians' experience of the city. How do the city's poorest residents understand modernist urban forms and their place within them? What do the built forms of the city evoke for them as possible futures, futures for themselves and for the city writ large? The makeshift way in which Monrovians

Major Sandi, Ministry of Defense. 2012. After the main eviction of squatters from the ministry building, Major Sandi was allowed to remain as a caretaker to the vast, empty property.

Major Sandi's quarters at the Ministry of Defense. 2012. Major Sandi's small room is now virtually the only evidence of human habitation in what was once a sprawling, crowded network of domestic spaces.

like Major Sandi occupy the city bears no resemblance to the vision of urban living that animated the design of the modern city, in Liberia or anywhere else. Monrovia, like the majority of capital cities across Africa and throughout the Global South, is a young city dominated by a built aesthetic conceived as a tool for progressive social transformation. While never uncontested (a point to which I return below), the modern movement and its architectural offshoots began as politically hopeful interventions for addressing the needs of cities seemingly ill equipped for industrialization, urbanization, and the "dream worlds" (Buck-Morss 2000) of totalizing economic systems. What Le Corbusier (2007) called the "new architecture" was intended to address the unmet need to accommodate and foster life in a very new age. Yet today many of Monrovia's youths inhabit spaces that they refer to in Liberian English as Monrovia's *gaps*: the ruins of public buildings, urban beaches, cemeteries, alleyways, parking lots, or dump sites. These gaps are created by a history of conflict, aging, and voluntary and involuntary neglect. But they are also created and re-created by the very form of the city itself. Though Liberia is one of the rare spaces on the African continent never to have fallen under a European colonial sovereign, its capital city is strewn with what Stoler (2013) has called "imperial debris": not just physical ruins, but ongoing, multifaceted processes of continued and active ruination. It is a fluid and unstable existence, but it is one shared by an alarming number of young Monrovians. This leads to a disturbing question: in this West African city, are those modernist ruins actually habitable today?

For many architects, planners, and designers, as for many anthropologists, sociologists, and journalists, the question that dominates the postmodern present is how to deal with the failure of those earlier mass utopian interventions. How do we make the modern city habitable for those who experience it primarily as a site of alienation and dispossession—largely thanks to the unworkability and eventual demise of modernist dreams? The goal is no longer to invent a new world of forms or to invent a new world through form. The goal is to learn to inhabit ruins. Hence a rash of early twenty-first-century literatures on the creativity and entrepreneurialism of squatters and slum dwellers (Koolhaas 2002; Neuwirth 2004); celebratory accounts of the temporary architectures of Occupy movements (Massey and Snyder 2012); and a fascination with urban invasions like the Torre David tower in Caracas (Urban Think Tank 2013) or Christiana in Copenhagen (Østervang 2008).

Facility converted from grain storage to condominiums, Copenhagen. 2013. In a pattern repeated in various forms in cities throughout the world, an obsolete industrial element on the city landscape—a ruin—has been repurposed as housing.

There are calls for a "transgressive architecture" (see Doron 2000) and calls for a "minor architecture" defined by the "making of spaces within the already built" (Stoner 2012: 16). Even architecture's mainstream adaptive reuse efforts are largely founded on the idea that the future of urban spaces can and should be crafted from existing forms, forms that would otherwise continue to exist principally as real or metaphoric ruins.

Such re-imaginings of ruin spaces are important efforts. They have helped, among other things, to tell the story of urbanism outside the relentlessly negative and ultimately unbelievable tropes that dominate how much of the world understands cities in Africa and across the Global South (Enwezor 2006; Robinson 2006). They have underscored the limitations of universal solutions and standards of value. They have highlighted hope and illuminated the many small challenges to hegemonic systems upon which it is possible to build.

The more celebratory case studies and manifestoes of building upon ruins, however, often underplay the meaning of *ruin* in its verb form: an ongoing process that names not just the devastated structures of the past but the "possibilities foreclosed" for imagining and crafting a different future (Stoler 2013: x). Both the material and immaterial detritus of violent histories in Monrovia exist as active forces on the urban landscape. They form boundaries and limits to what can be imagined and what can be done. Attending to the built environment not simply as the context for crafting an urban existence or as the raw material for inventing new urban forms requires a different, perhaps more pessimistic orientation. "Asking how people live *with* and *in* ruins redirects the engagement," Stoler argues, "to the politics animated, to the common sense such habitations disturb, to the critiques condensed or disallowed, and to the social relations avidly coalesced or shattered around them" (2013: 14).

My "redirected engagement" in *Monrovia Modern* concentrates on four structures in the Liberian capital. Each of these—the E. J. Roye Building, the Ministry of Defense, the Liberia Broadcasting System (LBS), and the Hotel Africa—embodies a modernist project that many Monrovians experience today as part of a ruined and ruinous landscape. As with all built forms, each of these sites is a web of physical spaces and narrative constructions, a material and immaterial aggregation that speaks to the relationship between the forms of the city and the lives of its inhabitants.

These histories are not self-contained. While they have unique aspects, they are of course linked to one another and to other urban forms. I use *form* here, and implicitly throughout this work, in Caroline Levine's (2015: 2) broad sense: forms are the work of making order. As such they travel the divide between material or immaterial, aesthetic and social. And as forms they have a politics; they are the condition of possibility for some ways of being in the city and a limiting factors in others. Reading these structures, I am also trying to read the structure of political possibilities and political limits. This is an effort to excavate from ruins a sense of the urban imaginary.

My detailed readings of these four sites on Monrovia's landscape are, of course, contiguous with other readings of Monrovia's everyday urbanism. Therefore, I bookend the four chapters devoted to these specific structures with other engagements with the modern city and its modernist legacies. The first is the most ethnographic of the chapters in *Monrovia Modern*. It is a reading of the politics of space and movement among the young men who made up the bulk of the population squatting in Monrovia's massive informal

E. J. Roye Building

Ministry of Defense

Liberia Broadcasting System

Hotel Africa

vertical settlements after the war. This first chapter is in some ways the anthropological foundation for the four photo-essays at the heart of the book. It presents an argument about the politics of habitation and dwelling that plays out somewhat differently in each iteration, but that nevertheless represents a common denominator in each of these spaces.

The concluding chapter takes the argument into the future city by asking how the modernist affordances of form that give meaning, or limit meaning, in the E. J. Roye, the Ministry of Defense, the LBS, or the Hotel Africa, came into play during the 2014–2015 Ebola outbreak in West Africa. The quarantines of Monrovia were surrounded by talk of extraordinary interventions in the policing of urban space at a time of crisis. At the same time, however, quarantine measures were in many ways the extension of a ruinous logic of habitation with which Monrovia's poor have dealt for a very long time—a logic that is legible in the existing built forms of the city.

In what remains of this introduction, I present the contextual background for the chapters that follow. I begin with a necessarily brief history of the instabilities of the city of Monrovia. This is followed by an equally cursory but nonetheless important overview of debates regarding the habitability of modernist architecture and design. These two discussions set up a third: the way African urbanism and its political possibilities have figured into the anthropological literature. Finally, I conclude with an explanation of the method of *Monrovia Modern*. Having relied heavily on what Dennis Tedlock (2013) calls a "photowriting" approach to understanding architecture and built form, I provide some background for thinking the tripartite relationship between word, image, and form in the anthropological study of architecture and the built environment.

Monrovia: Liquid City

The architect David Adjaye, in his omnibus survey of African cities, claims that "the feel of [Monrovia] is horizontal" (2011: 176), meaning that the life of the city is to be found on its streets and in its vast expanses of markets and microarchitecture rather than in tall buildings and the fixed geometries of urban design and planning. But the city's horizontal feel is also the product of a populace constantly on the move, shifting around the city in cyclical stop-start waves.

This has been true of Monrovia throughout its surprisingly short history as a city. As a name on the map, Monrovia has existed since 1822, when American former slaves and freemen built a permanent settlement at Cape Mesurado on the Saint Paul River.[1] Yet at the beginning of World War II, the population of Africa's oldest republic was still primarily rural; only 12,000 people were estimated to be living in its capital city (Lelong 1946, cited in Fraenkel 1964: 27).

A city that had been principally an administrative center and home port for Kru mariners expanded rapidly with the end of that war. By 1959 the population had grown to 53,000, and by 1989 to an estimated 600,000. The wartime expansion of Monrovia's port facilities (largely under the direction of the U.S. Army), along with President William Tubman's postwar open trade policies, radically increased the possibilities for up-country Liberians and foreigners to find work in Monrovia. A good deal of this labor was, however, seasonal, piecemeal, and casual. The disproportionately male populace of the city was highly mobile both within the city and around the region. The physical infrastructure of Monrovia, inadequate even for the small prewar population, came nowhere close to accommodating an influx of stevedores, construction workers, traders, and tradesmen. Though the city had a number of ethnic enclaves, even those permanently residing in the city often preferred temporary architecture because of the city's chaotic and ill-defined land tenure regimes and laissez-faire approach to housing controls (Fraenkel 1964: 52). Layered on top of a weak city government dominated by the patrimonial rule of the nation's president, such rapid but unstable growth gave much of the city a provisional, ad hoc feel. Merran Fraenkel, an anthropologist who conducted ethnographic research in the city in the late 1950s, describes "modern Monrovia" as a place that is "not really a town in the generally accepted sense of the word" but exists more as a "conglomeration of settlements and communities which participate to varying degrees in a common social and economic structure" (1964: 33).

Those infrastructure improvements to Monrovia enacted under President Tubman in the postwar years were heavily concentrated in the area of the city historically associated with its "civilized" residents, most notably (though not exclusively) with the Americo-Liberian elite.[2] Office complexes, bank buildings, cinemas, churches, mosques, and shopping centers were constructed on the high ridgeline downtown, looking out over the informal settlements and improvised architecture that made up most of the rest of the urban fabric.

The concentration of both modern design and concrete construction in the *kwiklo* (the so-called white man's town) was so predominant, in fact, that Samuel Doe's decision in the 1980s to build enormous, brutalist ministry buildings on the outskirts of the city was widely interpreted as an assault on Americo-Liberian hegemony (see Kaufmann 2016: 91). Visually, the skyline of Monrovia is dominated by this relatively small number of monumental, postwar modernist forms. But neither Tubman's nor Doe's building programs translated into a more stable urban environment for the bulk of Monrovia's residents in their everyday lives. Housing arrangements and housing stock remained largely informal, though this included a diversity of architectural styles as well as land occupation strategies.

Both the presence of squatters in the Ministry of Defense and their eviction therefore seem remarkably consistent, if somewhat exaggerated, urban logics in Monrovia. When war broke out in late 1989, up-country fighting and lack of economic options pushed many more people into a city that was no better equipped to accommodate them than it had been prior to the outbreak of violence. The city's populace of roughly 600,000 at the outset of the war reached as high as 1.5 million at the height of the conflict. By 2006, when an official UN resettlement program ended, there were still an estimated 1 million people living in the city. The Ducor Hotel, one of the city's most famous urban landmarks, was informally occupied for much of the war and for years afterward. The ministries of health and agriculture, at least three of the largest downtown banks, the national stadium, various political party headquarters, factories, beachside and suburban villas, and a major metropolitan hospital were all claimed as housing during the country's tumultuous decades of conflict. Informal settlements that were already crowded by the late 1950s became vastly more so in the 1990s, with little decrease in pressure since then. Phenomenologically, what this has meant is a city experiencing the effects of conflict not only as direct violence, but as a further compression of already shifting urban space.

Even a decade after the war, the majority of Monrovia's residents still have no clear title or demonstrable claim on the land they occupy, and tenure insecurity is a fact of life for most (see Williams 2011; as well as Hughes 2013). The laws governing rights of occupation in Monrovia remain unclear to most of the population, despite efforts to clarify the Liberian legal code's gray areas around squatters' rights and property disputes. Informal settlements continue to be the norm, though as the urban geographer Garth Myers (2011: 70–103) has argued, *informal* is a term that covers an unhelpful variety of habitation patterns in African cities today.

The Ellen Johnson Sirleaf government, which took power in Liberia in 2006, has brought with it a measure of political stability. With that stability, however, Monrovia has experienced urban growth of a different sort. Liberians who fled the war, which included a large number of wealthy and educated elites, are returning or remitting capital. Global financial institutions like the World Bank and International Monetary Fund are bankrolling development projects, as are a dizzying array of nongovernmental organizations (NGOs) and United Nations agencies. Multinational corporations trading in West Africa's natural resources and the financial industries that support that trade are all returning to a country that generates tremendous wealth for those willing to manage the risk. The influx of refugees and the internally displaced has thus been followed in postwar Monrovia by an influx of capital and "development-induced displacement" (see de Wet 2006; McDowell 1996).

The common thread that runs through both the wartime and postwar inflows is the way it lays claim to and shapes scarce urban space. Interventions in the built environment have happened quickly and with often dramatic, unpredictable results for the city's poorest residents. In the war's aftermath, the Monrovia City Corporation, which has primary responsibility for slum clearance along with the Ministry of Public Works, has received mixed reviews from NGOs and activists monitoring postwar land security issues (see, for example, Hughes 2013; Norton 2011; Williams 2011). By early 2012, there were efforts to regularize the way evictions were conducted and efforts to make them less militaristic. But large, sometimes violent sweeps of sectors of the city remain common. The chairman of the residents' association in Old Government Hospital, for example, claimed to have 137 families registered in the building when it was suddenly demolished in April 2012, at least some of them having lived in the building since the 1970s (Lupick 2012b). A significant portion of West Point, one of the largest and oldest settlements of the city with a population of some 60,000, was slated for demolition, and smaller slums were being bulldozed regularly. Many of these evictions and demolitions happened with little advance notice or relocation assistance. As Mary Broh, Monrovia's mayor, told one journalist in a 2012 interview: "As a postconflict country, we need to go through some rapid changes" (Lupick 2012a).

Ironically, then, even as the politics of Monrovia were becoming more stable, the physical space of the city became more unstable for many of its inhabitants. Monrovia, like many African cities, appears both to outsiders and to its residents as more liquid than solid. As the writer and critic Simon Njami puts it, describing African urban spaces in general, "It seems to me that as soon as one sets foot on the African continent, searching for the meaning of the city no longer refers in the least to any geometry, to any agreed and verifiable logic, nor to any urbanist ambition. It's no longer a question here of a physical city, with its street names, its signs, but of an intangible phenomenon" (2001: 72).

The liquidity of the city is perhaps most acutely experienced by the city's large population of men affiliated with the country's long war. Fighters from around the region have settled in Monrovia, a city widely seen by veterans of the Mano River war as more promising than Freetown, the capital of neighboring Sierra Leone, and easier to access for Anglophones than Conakry, Guinea, or Abidjan, Côte d'Ivoire.[3] By the UN's own conservative reckoning, the majority of that populace is living an extremely precarious existence. The final disarmament report frankly acknowledges something that is obvious to Monrovians: efforts at postconflict economic reintegration were largely unsuccessful, and social reintegration efforts were nonexistent.[4] For the country as a whole, unemployment and underemployment estimates of 70 to 85 percent circulate widely, with most accounts stressing that unemployment is disproportionately weighted toward Liberia's youth.[5] Monrovia is a rapidly changing landscape for all its residents, but arguably most of all for male residents who played some part in the 1990s regional war. As a result, large and small groups of men, many of whom fought together as units during the war, share temporary accommodations until forced out by police, by neighbors, or by fences and construction equipment.[6]

The irony of Njami's observation is that Monrovia, like many African cities, has for all its liquidity and intangible phenomena been profoundly shaped by the most rigid and tangible of geometries: the rationalism of modernist architecture and urban design. The spaces that make this horizontal city what it is—a fluid, liquid place of shifting forms and rapid displacements—are the product of a very different impulse and a seemingly contradictory history. It is to this history that I now turn.

Uninhabitable Architecture

For over half a century, the so-called international style has dominated not only Monrovia's but most African cities' skylines (see Elleh 1997: 72, 2002; Lepik 2013: 11). The early twentieth-century modernist movement and its many offshoots in architecture and urban design were a central, complex part of the colonial project in Africa (Avermaete, Karakayali, and Osten 2010; Fuller 2007; Rabinow 1989; Wright 1991), and in most cities played an equally important role in the nation-building and regime-building projects of the post-colonial era (see Chalfin 2014; Crinson 2003; Elleh 2002; Hess 2000, 2006; Larkin 2008). From the 1920s until arguably well into the 1980s, a great deal of the large-scale infrastructure of African cities was built with a strong commitment to the formal principles of modern design. More free to experiment in Africa than in Europe or North America, architects (African and non-African) could take modernist ideas to their extremes (Gogan and Rowley 2011). The clients for large-scale building projects in Africa (newly independent governments, religious institutions, and occasionally wealthy individuals) were eager for built forms perceived to be at the sophisticated cutting edge of global design.

As a result, Africa's cities are in fact among the world's most modern, at least as measured by the architectural aesthetics associated with high modernity. Certainly this was the case in Monrovia. Though never part of the European colonial empires, in Monrovia, modern nationhood meant modernism in the built environment (Olukoju 2006: 75).

In the broadest sense, in Africa as elsewhere, being modernist in design implied an architecture not bound by tradition, an architecture guided instead by the rational use of basic geometric forms to create new, functional spaces. Philip Johnson coined the term *international style* in 1932 to connote a global movement intended to be (like the industrial machines that often inspired modernist architects) an object whose style was no style at all. It would function free of cultural context or social influence.

Not surprisingly, then, the rhetoric surrounding the new architecture was often liberatory. Le Corbusier's famous dictum that the modern house was to be *la machine à habiter* [the machine for living or living in] was intended to reflect a new freedom through efficiency in form and function. Modernist architecture would harness and channel the productive forces of modernity itself: the labor power of industrial workers; the productive capacity of new domestic machinery like air conditioning and the electric oven; and mass-

Along UN Drive, Bushrod Island

produced building materials. It would take advantage of the radical new modes of seeing and thinking opened up by photography, and it would profit from the spaces of possibility (literal and figurative) created by the industrialization of modern war (see Cohen 2011; 2012: 16–17). The scale and abstract forms of structures like Le Corbusier's Unités d'habitation or the mass housing projects of Walter Gropius were intended to free workers (at least male workers) from the work of domesticity and habitation.

In reality, the history of modern architecture is more nuanced and conflicted. Despite its pretensions otherwise, it is inextricably linked to its sociohistorical contexts, especially the late nineteenth- and early twentieth-century expansion of industrial capitalism, colonial empires, and urban spaces. If its rhetoric was liberatory, the politics of the new aesthetic was not always progressive. A second Le Corbusier aphorism captures the ambivalent nature of at least some of the developing modern design ethos. In his 1922 *Vers une architecture*, perhaps the most influential tract of the early modern movement, Le Corbusier concludes by writing, "Architecture or revolution—revolution can be avoided" (2007: 307). The revolution Le Corbusier was primarily concerned with avoiding was a communist revolution inspired by the shortage and inadequacy of urban housing. It was not only in the colonies that the architecture of the modern movement was intended as a kind of pacification campaign.

There has therefore always been a concurrent debate as to whether modern architectural spaces are actually habitable. Thinkers on both the political left and right argued that the new architecture destroyed communities. The styleless style of the international style was for many a catastrophic loss of identity rather than a vehicle for realizing a new, more cosmopolitan future. Architectural modernism may have freed modern urbanites from tradition, but for many theorists it seemed to subject them to other, more subtle exercises of power and control.

For Walter Benjamin and Georg Simmel, for example, writing prior to World War II, the European city was experiencing the proliferation of spaces that were alienating, that forced urban residents to move through them without forming any real attachments or community. Benjamin famously wrote that modern Paris bred a new kind of subject, the flaneur or stroller who wanders the city observing his surroundings in minute detail but who remains unable to engage those surroundings fully (Benjamin 1978b; Buck-Morss 1986). For Simmel (1976), the modern city generated a "blasé attitude" of alienation and noncommitment, a product of the city's overwhelming population but also of its physical forms.

After World War II, critical evaluation of the impact of modern built forms was even more pessimistic. As Ian Buchanan and Greg Lambert put it, at least some theorists of the modern condition began to argue that modern spaces were "uninhabitable by definition" (2005: 3). The war's devastating impact on cities across Europe and Asia and the industrialized slaughter of the Holocaust, followed by the massive infrastructure projects needed to accommodate urban immigrants, workers, and refugees, suggested a built environment that could no longer consist of meaningful places, only of spaces of regulation, containment, and control. Architecture became a disciplinary

Downtown central business district, Monrovia. 2005. Like many African cities, the downtown core is dominated by international-style architecture.

tool, as Michel Foucault put it in his analyses of the modern European clinic, prison, and asylum. No one knew how to live in the spaces modernity had created. They were simply uninhabitable: "that state in which the modern subject no longer recognizes the space in which it is located" (Buchanan and Lambert 2005: 6).

Nowhere, perhaps, are the contradictory and confusing legacies of modern built forms more evident than in contemporary African cities. The most modern of cities, they have long been the laboratories of modernism's and modernity's successes and failures. The interventions have been especially sweeping, and the rhetoric of liberation especially pronounced. Like Monrovia, many of the continent's largest cities are in fact quite young, meaning their infrastructural development occurred almost wholly under the rubric

Unité d'habitation (Cité radieuse) #1

Unité d'habitation (Cité radieuse) #2

Le Corbusier's first *Unité d'habitation* (the *Cité radieuse*) at Marseille. 2014.
The revolutionary design of the *Cité radieuse* made it an icon—and an often
repeated model—for modern architects globally.

Unité d'habitation (Cité radieuse) #3

Unité d'habitation (Cité radieuse) #4

Unité d'habitation (Cité radieuse) #5

Unité d'habitation (Cité radieuse) #6

of modernist design technologies and principles (see Gandy 2014; Koolhaas 2002; Wainaina 2005). Ironically, then, it is the urban spaces least visible in the critical thinking about modernism and its legacies that provide the richest ground for understanding how urbanites live in modernism's spaces.

Thinking Africa's Urban Architecture

Debates about the habitability of urban form took on a particular cast in Africa south of the Sahara.[7] From the late 1930s until at least the 1970s, rapid urbanization in colonial southern Africa produced heated debates about the fate of ethnic identities as populations moved to the expanding cities, largely looking for work. Even for some anthropologists, the city seemed to be a major threat to an authentically African existence. To move to the city meant the loss of culture, the loss of identity, and the loss of social bonds to the (rural) tribe.

It was in the context of this debate that the South African Max Gluckman wrote one of the most-cited phrases in Africanist anthropology: "An African townsman is a townsman, an African miner is a miner: he is only secondarily a tribesman" (1960: 57). The city, he argued, did not simply erode the identities of those who occupied them. It created new forms of belonging and self-regard that were not limited by ethnicity. Ethnic identities continued to matter, but in the city one was always many things at once. It is what Gluckman said next, however, that I find most significant for thinking through the present moment in Monrovia: "That is, I would anticipate that as soon as Africans assemble in towns and engage in industrial work they will begin to form social relationships appropriate to their new situation: they will try to combine to better their conditions in trade unions and so forth" (1960: 57). For Gluckman and for others, the proliferating identities of the city inevitably produced new forms of collective living, and collective politics, that responded to specifically urban concerns. Facing the challenges of life in the city, urbanites would naturally find ways to make common cause and create a common identity around which to mobilize.

Indeed, the subsequent literature on associational life in African cities (mostly notably West African cities) is filled with accounts of how churches and mosques, ethnic associations, lending and social welfare societies, brotherhoods, hunting collectives, sports clubs, school groups, guilds, and fraternities all provided migrants to rapidly growing urban spaces with a social and

People's Movement for Democratic Change rally, Freetown, Sierra Leone. 2007.
Demonstrations in support of political parties remain the most visible instances of
collective popular action in this region of West Africa.

political framework within which to understand and participate in city life
(see, among many possible examples from this region alone, Cohen 1969,
1981; Fraenkel 1964; Little 1965, 1974; Nunley 1987).

The emphasis on multiplying identities and on the associational life that
springs from them has remained a central theme in studies of African urban
life long after the heyday of functionalism and structural Marxism. Much of
the more recent work on Pentecostalism in West Africa (see, for example,
Piot 2010; Quayson 2010; Shaw 2007a) is concerned with how the movement
provides a vocabulary of belonging in response to the almost impossible challenges of modern urban life. In contemporary Abidjan, anthropologist Sasha Newell (2012) describes how practices of conspicuous consumption and

largely fictional performances of wealth become techniques for cultivating a network of dependents and relations. Brian Larkin's (2008) ethnography of Nigerian cinema traces how both the symbolic and material spaces of the urban film industry work as sites for the creation of a modern Muslim identity and community (see also Meyer 1999). Associational life has hardly disappeared from the landscape of African urban studies; indeed, it has become richer and more complex as African cities have done so.

Yet at this moment, for many of its residents, the challenges of an African city life require such a proliferation of identities and performances that it becomes virtually impossible to imagine the city milieu generating the collective, transformative social and political movements through which to conceptualize and agitate for different rights to the city. The result is a landscape of remarkable inventiveness, but one in which it is exceedingly difficult to find solid ground for a common identity or project (see de Boeck 2013; Mbembe and Roitman 1995). Living in almost continuous crisis, a large proportion of young urbanites in Monrovia seem to survive by exploiting the fluid, provisional nature of relationships and identities in the city. There is little advantage in holding too tightly or too strictly to any one way of being or being known. For the ex-combatant men with whom I have spent the most time in Monrovia, all forms of identity become secondary, to use Gluckman's (1960) word: townsman and miner, along with youth, rebel, ex-combatant, student, man, Muslim, hustler, Pentecostal Christian, taxi driver, father, son, footballer, activist, NGO employee—as well as tribesman. Any identity may be foregrounded as necessary, along with the web of social relationships and social practices they invoke. But they are just as easily abandoned, sublimated, or renounced as circumstances require. In an urban milieu in which it can be difficult, even impossible, to predict which associations will be lasting or profitable, and which will be dangerous or fragile, all associations become provisional and contingent.

Urban associations forged by imaginative social bonds may, as Andrea Kaufmann (2016) has argued in her analysis of three civic associations in postwar Monrovia, provide a space for articulating modest expectations from the state. But such claims fall far short of a "political society" (Chatterjee 2004), as I take up in chapter 1. They make unstable material from which to form an effective political community. And in the post–Cold War era, the African state is itself a largely absent presence (see Mbembe 1992; Piot

2010), making it exceedingly difficult for oppositional coalitions to form and place demands. More often the collective activities of young urban men in this region have taken on the cast of the zero-sum, fantasmatic politics that the philosopher Achille Mbembe (2003) has described as a "necropolitics": practices of violence for profit and power, relationships of obligation and debt understood strictly according to the value systems of modern capitalism (see also Mbembe 2006). The idea of union factory workers mobilizing in the streets of Monrovia seems more fanciful than the mobilization of militias and mobs. Indeed the most common mass actions of young men in the past decades have been for the performance of wartime violence, or as political campaigners in the region's notoriously violent, cynical elections (see Christensen 2013; Christensen and Utas 2008; Hoffman 2011a).

Crucially, this shifting landscape of belonging also produces a remarkably dematerialized city. The associational life that interested Gluckman (1960) was one that could develop from recognizable, material spaces: mining hostels, factories, and churches, to name but a few of his examples. These were locations for specified activities and roles, a physical infrastructure that could facilitate the formation of a distinct kind of collective identity and action. But the more fluid, amorphous identities of Africa's city dwellers at this historical moment are accompanied by, and accomplished by, a more amorphous city. Urban forms seem to work against the kind of political coalition building that it was possible to imagine in the urbanizing southern African cities and towns that Gluckman invoked. As scholars such as Filip de Boeck (de Boeck and Plissart 2005), Simon Njami (2001), and AbdouMaliq Simone (2002) have put it, much of what constitutes the essence of the African urban fabric today is invisible. Literally invisible in many cases, as in the occult practices of urban residents or the unforeseeable consequences of people's gambles and entrepreneurial projects. But invisible also from the point of view of conventional urban design. Most of what urbanists know of the city simply fails to recognize the ways in which many urban Africans inhabit their built spaces (see Myers 2011; Pieterse and Simone 2013; Robinson 2006). City master plans, infrastructure projects, and even individual architectures, where they exist at all, are often put to use in ways they were never intended, and much of what matters in African urban life takes place in the gaps between those more recognizable, visible urban forms (Simone 2004: 22).

A new African urban literature has therefore begun to capture African urbanism's synthesis of movement, in/visibility, and experimentation. The productiveness of the city, for many of its inhabitants, is found in the creative ways they work these intersections and empty spaces. The materiality of the city becomes a backdrop to the city's more significant immaterial processes. Built forms function as raw material open to endless reworkings.

In a phrase that nicely captures the new urbanist thinking, de Boeck argues that the African city exists "beyond its architecture" (2011: 271; 2013: 95). In this dematerialized urban milieu, residents experiment with myriad ways to imagine and perform themselves. These are performances that take place in space, of course, but the result is a kind of "genericness" to many African cities (de Boeck 2013; see also Pivin 1999: 3). They become urban environments made up of spaces, not places, neither one thing nor another. Unformed spaces can be worked and reworked endlessly. Urban space becomes uncategorizable, neither public nor private in any of the usual senses.

It is a description apropos of modern Monrovia. There is certainly a genericness to much of the city, and the metaphors of liquidity are appropriate both materially and metaphorically. Monrovia's slums and interstitial spaces have their unique characteristics, but for the most part they are not spaces that invite different kinds of imaginaries about what it might mean to live there or what kind of people it is possible to become within them. Monrovia is a difficult city in which to find anchor points. Spaces in the city are interchangeable for many Monrovians, not least the young men who knew the city as a battle space during the war.

And yet there are forms in the city with histories and material aspects that have never been fully subsumed by the genericness of the rest of the city. Half finished or ruined, there are still locations in the city that, due to their material monumentality, their specific historical connotations, or their cultural or political significance, are not entirely tabula rasa for those who inhabit Monrovia today. These spaces may be subject to the same creative reworkings as every other space in the city. They host the same experiments in living and micromovements of habitation, but they resist being completely reduced to raw urban material. There are, in short, individual spaces in the city that it is impossible to exist "beyond." Many of these are forms that emerged directly from the global proliferation of the international style. It is not always easy to read those structures as architecture, given that so many exist in a state of ruin or at least neglect, and given the hyperbolic discourses that surround so

Downtown ruin, Monrovia. 2012. As in many West African cities, the boundaries that would demarcate public and private, boundaries that would give the city shape and structure, seem especially permeable.

much African urbanism.[8] But there are spaces of difference in Monrovia, as in all cities: forms that offer a unique purchase and perspective on the city, forms that exacerbate or challenge the city's dominant flows and trends. The modernist ideals they express may not, and generally do not, match the realities of the lives that people live within them. But as structures they give order to the urban world, an order that forecloses some possibilities for a future even as it opens others.

Understanding the spaces in the city that it is impossible to live beyond means attending to individual forms and their particularities. The chapters that follow therefore present this argument vis-à-vis microanalyses of specific ruins and the possibilities that those ruins both enable and foreclose. Like all analysis of architecture, and indeed all analysis of African urban life, it is an exploration deeply enmeshed in the politics of representation. And so I conclude this introduction by thinking specifically about the photo-essay approach that animates the chapters to follow.

Photowriting the Built Environment

In photojournalist Tim Hetherington's book *Long Story Bit by Bit: Liberia Retold*, the Ministry of Defense building sits like a reprimand in the midground of a single image. The photograph was made in 2006, three years after the war ended. Only a fraction of the structure is visible: an imposing corner tower and part of one façade. The building takes up a third of the frame. Another third is ominous gray sky, the rest lush tropical bush. What is visible of the building's face is enough to show how squatters have hung reed mats and cardboard to form makeshift walls on two floors. The ad hoc patterns underscore the improvised, parasitic nature of their construction (2009: 72–73). It is a powerful image and reads, as do many others of urban infrastructure in the book, as an indictment. It is a photograph of ruins, but like all representations of ruins its meaning is difficult to pin down (Hell and Schönle 2010: 6). The object of Hetherington's critique could be war and the ruination that has forced Monrovians to seek out clearly inadequate shelter. It could be the disastrous and unsustainable politics of patrimonialism that resulted in such inappropriate forms. It could be a critique of Africa itself.

Photographs of the built environment, whether classified as architectural photography, reportage, fine art, or snapshot, always present an argument. They are a "provocation," as Jane Tormey (2013) puts it. Though frequently thought of as the most anodyne and banal of photographic genres, architectural photographs are never mere illustration. Like Hetherington's Ministry of Defense image, what photographs of architecture argue may be ambiguous or ambivalent. But the combination of content, aesthetic, technology, and context that makes up the photograph, both inside and outside the frame, are invariably evidence in a case for, or against, something.

At what point, however, does that visual evidence become anthropological evidence? More and more frequently that term circulates around an approach to photographing the built environment that attempts a break with the strict formalism of traditional architectural image making. Iwan Baan, the Dutch photographer whose reportage aesthetic has made him one of the most celebrated contemporary architectural photographers, is routinely described as performing a kind of anthropological analysis with his images of informal settlements, modernist icons, and aerial cityscapes, as well as his documentary work for global architecture firms (*Artweek.LA* 2013; Häntzschel 2013; Schim van der Loeff 2014). South African Guy Tillim's documentary photographs of

Johannesburg apartment blocks and the colonial modern architecture of central Africa is similarly described as social analysis (see, for example, Enwezor 2010). Calling these approaches to architectural photography anthropological seems to be shorthand for images that include people and show how they occupy built space. But architectural photographs, whether they are populated or not, have always been anthropological, have always been ethnographic. They always theorize, more or less explicitly, a relationship between human beings and the forms that surround them. The more important question, then, is not at what point does photography of the built environment become anthropology, but what kind of anthropological arguments can architectural photography make? One answer to that question can be found at the intersection of two legacies of the photograph: its role in defining the improbable, sometimes impossible space of modernist architecture, and its role in defining the improbable and sometimes impossible place of African modernity.

Photography has arguably been the most important technology in the development of modern architecture. The medium's portability means that most people's experience of canonical structures, including most architects' experience of them, comes from photographs rather than from the direct experience of space itself. Modern designers learned about new works, and developed their theoretical and philosophical positions, through circulating photographs of built forms from around the globe.[9] Their own designs were therefore a response not only to other architecture but to the peculiarity of how the still camera renders architectural space.

The results could be dramatic. Claire Zimmerman has, for example, argued that the widely circulated professional photographs of Mies van der Rohe's Tugendhat House in Brno (in what is now the Czech Republic) led this rather unusual and unrepresentative example of Weimar modernism to become the signature, frequently imitated aesthetic of global modernist architecture. Photographed in the early 1930s, the images have to be understood as the product of multiple technical and aesthetic determinants: the wide-angle lens's tendency to warp space, especially midground space, making elements in the background appear condensed and farther from the camera; contemporary pictorial landscape painting conventions that favored strong foreground elements, a middle void, and crowded backgrounds; and the predominant focus in the images on the open common areas of the house rather than the smaller private spaces. The result is a peculiar rendering of modernism, a rendering that overemphasizes compositional symmetry, openness, and transparency while underemphasizing the experiential qualities of occupying space. It is a modernism dominated by the pictorial qualities of looking from a fixed point of view. Especially as it spread globally, the image of modern architecture increasingly became the image of modern architecture as depicted in still photography. Architects working in the modern mode were in dialogue with a distorted image of the object they hoped to produce: "Internationalism in architecture was," Zimmerman concludes, "the result of photographic circulation and its concomitant modes of cursory and inattentive seeing" (2004: 349).

In some cases, the camera's role in turning impossible spaces into ideal modernist space is even more central. Le Corbusier's *Vers une architecture* is richly illustrated with photographs of modern machinery, vehicles, and industrial buildings from early twentieth-century America. But his images of grain silos, one of his quintessential exemplars of pure functional geometry, were doctored for publication. Service elements that make the building work but that distract from its purity of shape were removed from the image in the darkroom. The versions printed in the book appear much more elemental and abstract than their originals on New England farmscapes and the plains of the American Midwest (see Brown 1993; Steiner 2006: 108).

In short, the image of modern movement architecture is in many ways a uniquely photographic image. Inhabiting the spaces of modernism is in large measure a process of learning to inhabit spaces crafted by and for the camera's, rather than the human body's, unique relationship to built forms.

The camera not only played a central role in creating the spaces of modernism. It also played a central role in the debate over what it might mean to live in those spaces. The photographs of Mies's Tugendhat House helped precipitate what is, according to Zimmerman (2004: 343–345), often referred to as the "Can one live in the Tugendhat House?" debate. Critics and supporters of the building's design disagreed whether the materials, lines, and most of all the spatial arrangements of the architecture were a liberating advancement or a dehumanizing misintepretation of what it meant to dwell at home. But while each side included advocates who had actually been in the building, for the most part the debate was staged around interpretations of photographs of the building's interiors, photographs that, as Zimmerman explains, are remarkably unfaithful to the experience of the place. Julius Shulman (1997), one of the most renowned architectural photographers of the midcentury modernist period, has described his role in producing images like that of two women suspended over the Los Angeles nightscape as part of a project of convincing viewers that the spaces of modern architecture were actually habitable. Ernie Braun's intimate scenes of domestic life in advertising images for the famous Eichler homes in California, among the first mass-produced modernist housing, were meant not only to sell the homes but to instruct homeowners in how to use their unfamiliar spaces (Adamson, Arbunich, and Braun 2002). Photography, in other words, played as much a role as the built environment in structuring the imagination of what kinds of spaces were habitable and how in modern architecture.

A parallel argument has run long and deep in African studies: that Africa and Africans are largely understood, by those both outside and on the continent, through images—often impossible images. Okwui Enwezor (2006: 12) starkly summarizes the argument when he writes, in his introduction to the *Snap Judgments* catalog of African photography, that the dominant images of Africa, images of unrelenting misery or untrammeled natural beauty, are simply "no longer plausible" after decades of repetition. Like the image of modern architecture, the image of modern Africa takes on a kind of hyperreality, a signifier without referent, more real than the thing to which it supposedly refers.

Here, too, the critique is more than semantic. There are material consequences to this political economy of the photograph. Young men who participated in the wars in Sierra Leone and Liberia did so not only as combatants but as media consumers. They understood in a sophisticated way that they participated in a global economy of image production and dissemination. Many of their techniques and strategies for the performance of violence can and should be understood as efforts to reproduce images of themselves as modern African warriors in a crowded mediascape with clearly defined ideas of what African violence looks like. It is, however, an image that largely divorces violence from its consequences, or at least from its politics (see Hoffman 2004, 2011b; as well as Richards 1996).

While arguably the hyperreality of images in the Mano River war makes it among the first truly postmodern conflicts, it is of a piece with a much deeper history of photography in Africa as the arbiter of the modern. Magazines like *Drum* and the advertising images of billboards and newspapers, for example, have long used photography to promote an image of the modern African

Julius Shulman photographing the Stahl House, Case Study House #22. Photo credit: J. Paul Getty Trust.

subject as a particular kind of consumer, an image intertwined with the social injustices of colonialism, apartheid, and economic inequalities (see, for example, Burke 1996; Thomas 2006). Studio portraiture has been a privileged site for exploring what it meant, and continues to mean, to be a modern African and what it means to share or be excluded from other people's modernity (see, for example, Lamuniere 2001; Matt and Mieβgang 2001; Mofokeng 2012; Oguibe 2001). The still camera has, in short, long been a key technology in writing the story of what kinds of modernity are possible and what kinds impossible across the continent.

Both of these genealogies of photography and modernity, the one distinctly architectural and the other distinctly African, inform my own process of "photowriting the built environment," as the anthropologist Dennis Tedlock (2013) puts it. The fact that prose writing and photographic production now rely on so many of the same technologies, according to Tedlock, has further eroded the disciplinary boundary between media. A long-held notion that each medium requires specialist competencies that a single author cannot master is crumbling. It is increasingly possible to pair the two and employ their individual communicative and analytic potential in a single coherent essay, one that need not necessarily prioritize one medium over the other. And where the object of photowriting's inquiry is the human experience of place, the built environment holds special potential, "replete with the echoes, traces, and results of speaking, writing, and other human acts that have taken place within that world" (Tedlock 2013).[10]

Chapters 2–5 of *Monrovia Modern* are each devoted to a single structure, and each employs a photowriting methodology. Each package of text and images therefore consists of a selection of photographs that deploys the camera's unique ability to render space and to reflect how photography shaped the modernist imaginary of architectural form. What's more, they are images imbued with the legacy of photography on the continent, images haunted by older images of what African modernity should be. They are, in that sense, double provocations (to return to Tormey's term). They make visible the "photographicness" of modern movement design and the political economy of images in African urbanism.

While I am content to have those provocations, the arguments of the images, be somewhat open-ended, there is a logic to how the images are selected and organized. It is a logic that I believe requires some explication. At the end of each chapter, then, I have used a short postscript to outline my own readings of these photo packages. Without attempting to foreclose the excess of meaning inherent in ethnographic images (Taylor 1996: 75; Sniadecki 2014: 26), I nevertheless recognize that a certain amount of framing would increase, rather than diminish, a reader's ability to divine meaning within these frames (see Desjarlais 2015: 214).

TAKEN TOGETHER, THESE CHAPTERS present a portrait, albeit a partial one, of the political imaginary and its relation to urban form. They do not offer a yes or no answer to the question of whether Monrovia's modernist ruins are habitable. They are intended, rather, to probe the limits of what a city's residents can think and do with the form of the city in which they live. Together these chapters constitute an anthropology of the forms of Monrovia's modernism. They are a mapping of the city's imperial debris.

CHAPTER 1

Live Dangerously, My Brothers
Ex-Combatants and the
Political Economy of Space

Darvin

It was hard to know just what to make of Major General Human Garbage. Things grew even more confusing when he took off running after Junior Senator Peanut Butter. "Hey, man!" he screamed. "Hey, man! Stop the car! I want to talk to you!" Human Garbage caught up with Peanut Butter's black Jeep Cherokee just as it reached the main road, banging on the doors until the senator rolled down the window and gave Human Garbage a minute of his time. Soon Human Garbage was back, ready to continue his strange tale.

Human Garbage, or Arthur Kollie, looked older than most of the other young men in the small Monrovia enclave of Congo Town Back Road. This, it turned out, was not actually the case. Hard living had simply aged Human Garbage faster than the others. But like all those who squatted here, he was a former military man with the Government of Liberia forces, the constellation of security units under former rebel turned Liberian president Charles Taylor. Human Garbage (he insisted on being called by his nom de guerre) was a little unclear as to whether he was an officer of rank in the Armed Forces of Liberia or a member of one of Taylor's less formal militias. But he proudly boasted that right up to the day that Charles Taylor left Liberia for exile in August 2003, he drew a salary of 10,000 Liberian dollars every month (approximately U.S. $200 at the time). He had two stars, two jeeps, a wife, and girlfriends. He had a house not far from Charles Taylor's own residence, White Flower. In fact it was the house that gave Human Garbage his name.

EJ ROYE FROM
PAST NEW BRIDGE

Field sketch #1, E. J. Roye Building

When his unit was involved in killing Taylor's enemies, at least a few of the bodies, the "human garbage," were buried in Arthur Kollie's backyard.

The day I met him in April 2012, however, Human Garbage seemed more a clown than a respected military man. He approached as I interviewed ex-combatants at Congo Town Back Road. "Here I am! Major General Human Garbage!" he said, standing at attention stiff and very close. He was dressed in a black suit coat with no shirt. "Great! We have been expecting you!" I shouted back at him, assuming (neither correctly nor incorrectly, as it turned out) that after a day filled with stories of human drama we were now in the realm of social parody.

The half-dozen young men to whom I had been speaking greeted Human Garbage much the same way. "The great Human Garbage is here!" "Oh, my major general!" It was all the encouragement he needed. "I am a major general. Human Garbage. Everyone knows me. Everyone. Even the smallest child. That boy over there, he knows me. Only the smallest babies don't know me. But you can come here and say 'Human Garbage' and everyone will know me."

Arthur Kollie, aka Human Garbage. Once a respected fighter with Charles Taylor's forces, in 2012 Kollie survived by breaking rocks into gravel with a group of other ex-combatants in the Congo Town Back Road community.

That's when the black SUV bumped down the road behind us. One of the men pointed to it. "That's General Peanut Butter. You know him?" I did, though only by reputation. Adolphus Dolo, or Peanut Butter (now Junior Senator Peanut Butter), was a prominent figure in the National Patriotic Front of Liberia (NPFL). In the post-Taylor period he was elected junior senator from Nimba County. Unlike Human Garbage, post-Taylor Liberia had been good to Dolo. Along with a handful of other top NPFL commanders, he had amassed substantial holdings in land and real estate, in both Monrovia and Nimba County.

Seeing the vehicle, Human Garbage took off. When he returned, he insisted I follow him to see his current residence.

Together we trudged up the hill behind the newly renovated Ministry of Health building, where Human Garbage and hundreds of other fighters squatted for more than seven years after Taylor's ouster. It was a building that its residents aptly named Titanic, referring to its prow-like tower as well as its fate: "It was sinking and so were we," as one former resident put it. Since their eviction, Human Garbage and other members of his unit have been living behind the building, breaking rocks into gravel and mining sand from the beach for sale to local builders.

Human Garbage led the way to the skeletal remains of a house that had long since lost its roof, windows, and most of its walls. We passed a young woman with a baby at her feet, and Human Garbage picked up the child. "This is my woman," he said, without greeting her or even slowing his pace. "And this is my child."

Pulling back a curtain on one of two rooms in what had been a small outbuilding, he stepped back. "And this is my house." The room was small but clean. Stacked on the shelves was a surprisingly large collection of stuffed animals. Nicely laundered clothes hung on the walls. The ex-combatants who had followed us up the hill began to laugh. "Major General, why don't you get a picture in your house!" One of them grabbed Human Garbage and dragged him to the tiny structure's other room. A piece of wood bravely covered part of the doorway. Inside was a filthy mattress surrounded by tattered clothes. The fighters pushed Human Garbage inside, and he grimly sat on his bed. This, the other ex-combatants explained, is where Human Garbage actually lived. The baby was not his child and the woman was his neighbor, not his wife. Human Garbage had done his best to give himself some momentary measure of visibility as a man with a home and family, albeit a modest one on both counts. But Human Garbage, it turned out, had nothing.

"Can you imagine?" said one of the fighters as we left. "The man had two stars, two jeeps. Women. Now Human Garbage doesn't even have a door."

Human Garbage's case crystallizes the complexities of life in Liberia's capital city for the men who joined Charles Taylor's "revolution," served in the security apparatus of his warlord state, or fought against those same forces in the 1990s and early 2000s. A few have thrived in the post-Taylor city. But in Monrovia in early 2012, there are many more young men who resemble Human Garbage than who resemble Peanut Butter.

Most ex-fighters have found no fixed place in what we might call the formal or legible city: few were incorporated into the post-Taylor state security

FACING PAGE: Arthur Kollie's house. The small outbuilding in which Kollie lives sits close to two of his former residences: his wartime villa and the Ministry of Health building in which he squatted for years.

apparatus; the disarmament and reintegration program (the DDRRP) failed to give them entrée into the wage labor economy; most have no stable housing and no reliable guarantees to whatever land they occupy; ex-combatants have ambiguous standing vis-à-vis the police and the juridical order of the city. And yet even as they are excluded from the formal city, these young men are subject to its logic at every turn. They live in a "relational city" (Pieterse 2008; see also Myers 2011: 16), an urban regime in which planning at multiple scales and at multiple degrees of formality intersects to create the lived realities of Africa's urban space.

The relationship I trace in this chapter is triangular. It connects young male ex-fighters to the built environment of the city and to some kind of imagined urban future. In the chapters that follow I examine in greater detail the limits and possibilities of four specific forms on the urban landscape and explore the kinds of urban futures they both make possible and foreclose. It is a project of excavating what Stoler (2013: ix) has called "imperial debris," the "foreclosed possibilities" that result from living among ruins. Understanding that process, however, requires a more general understanding of the urban spaces and forms with which and within which many young Monrovians live. The male youth who participated in this region's long decade of armed conflict are not exceptional among young people, though often the dramatic rise and fall of their fortunes is especially illuminating of the wider processes of the city.

"Live dangerously, my brothers." That line from Friedrich Nietzsche's *The Gay Science* was underlined by the architect Le Corbusier (Charles-Edouard Jeanneret) in his copy of the philosopher's work (Cohen 1999: 318). "Build your cities on the slopes of Vesuvius! Send your ships into uncharted seas! Live at war with your peers and with yourself!" (Nietzsche 1974: 228; cited in Cohen 1999: 328). For both men, this passage seemed to be a call to imagine different and difficult ways to exist. Le Corbusier certainly saw his new architecture as a way to live dangerously, a way for built form to serve as the catalyst for inventive modes of inhabiting the city, a machine for producing new possibilities in living and dwelling.

Human Garbage and thousands of young men like him live dangerous lives in Monrovia, dangerous both in the pedestrian sense and in this more evocative spirit of inventiveness that Le Corbusier found so appealing. Theirs is a métier of war and of sailing uncharted seas. But strangely this inventiveness was constricted by a limited imagination. Ex-combatants like Human Garbage or the other inhabitants of Titanic, Congo Town Back Road, or Monrovia's other *ghettoes* (used here as a Liberian English term) seemed incapable of thinking of their own practices of invention as ones upon which they could build collective identities or through which they could articulate collective demands, let alone invent new kinds of space or new forms of urban citizenship. Those possibilities seemed always foreclosed by the city they knew, a city that seemed to make truly revolutionary, dangerous living impossible.

Spaces of Invention

There are only two fixed landmarks in the eastern Monrovia sector known as Zimbabwe: the taxi rank on UN Drive and the Truck Inn bar behind it. A patchwork of houses, individual rooms, bamboo shelters, alleys, and footpaths extends out from these spaces, but it is a constantly shifting landscape. What spaces make up Zimbabwe depends on who inhabits them at any given moment, and Zimbabwe itself only exists for a small population of ex-combatants, their families and friends.

Koffi is the senior man at Zimbabwe. The neighborhood, he says, took its name from the headlines: Robert Mugabe's campaign of land seizures, violent evictions, and house demolitions held considerable interest for Liberians. With the same blend of irony and homage common to young men in urban spaces around Africa (see Weiss 2002), the residents of Zimbabwe found a way to name both their marginality and their respect for the absoluteness of power that helped to make them that way.

Koffi fought first with Samuel Doe in the 1980s, then with the United Liberation Movement for Democracy in Liberia, and finally with Liberians United for Reconciliation and Democracy (LURD), meaning he was at war for some fifteen years. Most of the young men who live in Zimbabwe were part of his unit in one or more of these factions, and all now need at least his tacit permission to be in Zimbabwe or to "go on operations" from there. Koffi estimates that dozens of his boys sleep in Zimbabwe on any given night, though in truth for most of them Zimbabwe is only one of a handful of spaces around the city in which they might stay for a few hours, a few days, perhaps longer.

In the postwar city, the operations on which they deploy primarily involve running errands, transporting goods across town in a wheelbarrow, changing

Nightscape, Zimbabwe (Bushrod Island). 2010. The neighborhood is ephemeral. Its physical infrastructure is constantly shifting, as is its populace and its place in the geography of the city.

currency, or, most lucratively, jacking cell phones from the taxi rank. Roland, an ex-LURD fighter in his early thirties, explains the latter process over beers at the Truck Inn. Young men hang around the taxi rank offering to load goods and passengers for crosstown or up-country transport. Or they sit in front of the bar, more or less blending into the dense fabric of money changers and petty traders that occupy the periphery of the taxi rank. When the opportunity presents itself, a man will grab one of the ubiquitous cell phones of a taxi passenger. The thief then sprints into the bar and out the other side, disappearing into Zimbabwe.

Savvy Monrovians know what to do next. They quickly approach the money changers or a member of the Neighborhood Watch Committee. "Being that the place is a ghetto," Roland explains, "and the police come from far away and don't know the area, they are not really active here." So the police have outsourced security to the watch committee, who like the moneychangers are primarily ex-combatants. On any given day, Zimbabwe's ex-combatant populace might play any one of these roles: money changer, baggage handler, watch committee member, thief.

The chain of events that follows depends to a large degree on the finances of the robbery victim and the various parties' powers of argument and negotiation. Watch committee representatives or the assembled moneylenders suggest that they might be able to locate the thief on the victim's behalf. If the victim is in a hurry and would prefer to simply buy back her phone, and to reward the intermediary for his time and effort, the whole business can be settled in a matter of minutes. For a lesser price the target could buy back his SIM card and forgo the phone, at least for now. If he waits a day and then stops at the downtown market known locally as Buy Your Own Things, he might get lucky and find his phone (or someone else's) at a better price.

It is a thin façade, this shifting landscape of players and roles. Only one part of the performance is nonnegotiable: the aggrieved party cannot personally enter Zimbabwe in pursuit of the thief. For them it is a no-go area. For them Zimbabwe doesn't exist.

African urbanism has, as Simone (2001, 2002) puts it, fractured the logical correlations between cause and effect. The flows of wealth, people, and information are too chaotic and unpredictable to chart linear paths through space or time. City life in many quarters of contemporary African cities has therefore become a métier of experimentation in which storytelling, bluffing, and the scam are, at least for many young men, quintessential urban practices. Young people in particular must invent their own outcomes and the performances through which they hope to realize them. In the garbage dump across the highway from Zimbabwe, for example, there is a young man who for the past few weeks has been patrolling the edges of the dump in a uniform stolen from a private security company. He was once a member of some branch of Charles Taylor's armed forces, though he has long been out of government employ. Periodically, however, he arrests someone, and the residents of the area occasionally call him in to settle disputes. He is reasonably good at working through the issues at hand, and he charges less to dispense justice than do the actual police at the station nearby. His is an extreme example, but it is an extremity only of degree.

As scholars of other African cities have shown, urban practices of invention are often practices of the body. Young men in Kinshasa and Brazzaville, for example, use designer clothing to mark themselves as cosmopolitan and worldly, even if doing so leaves them virtually penniless (MacGaffey and Bazenguissa-Ganga 2000; Pype 2007; Thomas 2003). In his ethnography of Abidjan's *bluffeurs*, Newell (2012) describes how male youths put any surplus resources toward luxury goods and bar tabs, creating an obviously performed image of themselves as wealthy men capable of consuming without care. In photographer Philip Kwame Apagya's Ghana portraits, young people have themselves photographed against backdrops of the New York skyline or with expensive domestic appliances, visualizing themselves in places they have never been and with goods they do not own (Mießgang 2001; Wendl 2001; see also Behrend 2013; Oguibe 2001). It is not that people are unaware that these fantastic images are unreal. It is that phantasms can, and often do, bring about new realities for those who perform them.

What Zimbabwe suggests is that in Monrovia, at least, these practices of invention are also practices of space. For postwar Monrovia, the ex-combatant population's opportunities to participate in even meager displays of conspicuous consumption are limited. What they cannot accomplish through the circulation of commodities young men attempt through physical movement and speed. Ex-combatants in Monrovia tend to disperse themselves around the city. They circulate between urban spaces to seize or generate emergent opportunities.

Hassan is a good example. It is hard to say where Hassan lives. His knowledge of Monrovia is encyclopedic. He has a few personal effects stored in dwellings across the city, many of them loaned to friends or kin, others borrowed from them. The unspoken terms of these material exchanges are that Hassan can expect a meal or place to sleep as need or circumstances prescribe. The result is a wide social net that Hassan maintains by physically traveling its threads through the city, cultivating contacts and exploiting opportunities as he goes. As we moved together across Monrovia, Hassan continuously scanned the surrounding landscape, seeking out faces he knew, occasionally making a quick change of course to catch one person's eye or to avoid another. He routinely hailed familiar faces on the street, often with vague gestures or promises to return at an unspecified time in the future. It was an elaborate game that Hassan played better than most. Movement had become a profession for Hassan, a kind of centrifugal force out of which he could generate profits and occasional success.

The urban spaces that Hassan and other ex-combatants frequent extend beyond the confines of the city proper and into the peri-urban peripheries. A short drive west of Monrovia lies the remains of the Guthrie rubber plantation. Occupied during and after the war by a large group of LURD fighters, the plantation has since been purchased by a Malaysian corporation that has uprooted most of the rubber trees. In their place they have planted palm saplings, hoping to capitalize on a booming international market in palm oil.

Rubber tapper, former Guthrie Plantation. 2005. The plantation housed a large ex-combatant population for years after the war. With the spike in global palm oil prices, much of the plantation has been purchased by foreign companies and converted to palm production.

I find Small Dennis there with a group of fighters in a makeshift camp. It is the last of what was once a sizable population of ex-combatants who hid among the trees, refusing to disarm or to acknowledge that the war was over.[1] When they are in the plantation, Small Dennis's men live together in three huts made of palm fronds and burlap sacks tucked into one of the remaining rubber tree groves. Dennis rents a room in a hut nearby. One of the women in the tiny village does some cooking and washing for the young men when they can afford it.

The Guthrie Plantation is no one's preferred dwelling place. Dennis spends a good deal of his time here, but is often further up-country working the gold and diamond mines of the Sierra Leone–Liberia border or at one of his posts in Monrovia. His boys are similarly mobile, working their way through networked spaces that are always a compromise, always a gamble. At Guthrie the work is every bit as hard as the mines and the potential payoffs much smaller. But it is closer to the city center and the spaces that matter there. Men come to the plantation to earn something small, and having done so they can continue on their way. "If you have money, you go to Monrovia," shrugged one young man. "If you don't have money, you stay here."

In the huts of Small Dennis's crew. 2012. The make-shift dwellings fit the mobility of the young men who inhabit them but belie the semipermanence of squatters on the plantation grounds.

Small Dennis's circulating crew of youths are well known to the Malaysian plantation owners. A few have been hired as security guards. Most, however, are allowed to stay on the plantation grounds as a kind of "reserve industrial army" (Marx [1867] 1977: 784–786). The company hires them on occasion to dig holes for new palm saplings or perform other manual labors. In exchange for keeping an eye on the valuable young palm trees, the new owners prefer not to notice when Small Dennis and his crew illegally tap rubber from the remaining trees or mine sand from the nearby riverbed for sale in the city. For Dennis and the others, this is an easily accessible node in a network that spans the breadth of the city, a forest redoubt in which they are thieves or security guards, workers or rebels as circumstances allow. For the company it doesn't matter who occupies the forest camp or how they think of themselves, provided they abide by the few tacit rules of this parasitic relationship. Seemingly wild and unregulated, the Guthrie forest camps are in fact the perfect crystallization of what Gilles Deleuze once called the "society of control": a space in which identities are irrelevant, a space in which power and profit are derived not from knowing (or caring) who occupies a space but simply from knowing where bodies can be found (see Deleuze 1995; Hardt 1995: 36).[2]

Fumba Konneh's diamond miners. 2012. The mines closest to Monrovia have been worked numerous times, but remain part of the urban constellation through which ex-combatants orbit.

Almost equidistant to the north, Fumba Konneh has made a different bet with the forest at the city's edge. Like Dennis, he controls a small group of ex-fighters. They, too, make the trip from the urban center to the peri-urban periphery with great frequency. There they live in the dense bush that has overtaken what was once a large sugar cane production and refining facility. By the 1980s the production facility had closed. Most of the byroads that connected the region to Monrovia proper have crumbled, as have all but the most skeletal remains of the industrial infrastructure. Just before the war, the site was extensively mined for gold and diamonds, and the depressions of this earlier mining activity are still visible on the forest floor.

Fumba Konneh doesn't know how successful these earlier mines were. But he knows how to read the signs of the forest and has consulted diviners. There must, he believes, still be gems in the old pits and so he and his men are once again scraping and flooding the forest floor. The payoff is unlikely to be large, certainly smaller than what they might find in the mines along the border. But proximity to the city means his costs are less and logistics easier. He can bring in men he doesn't know well to dig the pits and recruit former comrades in arms for the more delicate task of washing the gravel in pursuit of stones. He need not care for those who grow sick or are injured deep in the forest. For the miners themselves, peri-urban sites mean that digging can be casual labor and that what little they may earn can be put into circulation with relative ease.

This is, then, a political economy built on movement. The extent to which the ex-combatants living in spaces like Zimbabwe, Guthrie, and the peri-urban mining zones understand this is exemplified by a strange kind of nostalgia for the war years. For at least some ex-combatants, peace is primarily a state of being that has limited their ability to move. The threat of returning to war is one that haunts many conversations in Monrovia today. While very few claim to want war, an alarming number claim that were it to return to the region they would unhesitatingly join the effort, regardless of cause or purpose.[3] It is a language that tends to be spatialized; returning to war is often depicted as an act of relocating from where one is at present. "My brother, I will not lie," said one of Small Dennis's lieutenants. "If I give the word, a thousand men will leave this forest." War is always an elsewhere, a worlding of opportunities, a chance to leave this place in which one risks being stuck.[4] Askari, a man whose own wartime circuit included Liberia, Sierra Leone, and Guinea, succinctly captured the perverse cosmopolitanism he and other young men perceived in the region's instability. Forced to move, the "backward" people of Liberia learned to do new things and to think in new ways. War created opportunities for combatants and noncombatants alike because it propelled people into new spaces where they were forced to invent for themselves new possibilities. "War," as he summarized his argument, "is useful for movement."

It is important to recognize, however, that these fighters' nomadism is limited to certain kinds of spaces. The city for them is an agglomeration of spaces of invention, liquid spaces the boundaries and composition of which were themselves constantly in motion. But the city as a whole is not smooth space, to use a Deleuzian term for landscapes that foster experimentation and the undoing of dominant codes and regimes (Deleuze and Guattari 1987: 351–423) . The city was not a tabula rasa. Not every space is a space of invention for ex-combatants piecing together circuits of navigation and movement. Ex-combatants' maps of the city tend to consist of particular kinds of spaces: ruins, dumping grounds, beachfronts, taxi ranks, and parking lots. For all of the apparent freewheelingness and liquidity of the urban milieu in

Ex-combatants' shacks and boats outside West Point. 2012. Among the fishing fleet at the West Point slum in Monrovia are several boats belonging to a LURD ex-commander who stole them up-country, then moved to Monrovia to begin a small fishing operation.

which they maneuver, most often young men find themselves in urban spaces of a particular form—a form that also imposes real limits on what their vision of city life could be.

Life in the Gap

The consensus among ex-combatants at the Duport Road Cemetery is that about a hundred youths live there. Most are men, though a few female sex workers spend at least some of their nights among the graves. The majority once had spaces in Titanic or squatted in the Ministry of Defense. Now about half of the group keep at least some of their belongings in the graveyard.

The marijuana trade brings a small amount of cash to the populace at Duport Road. Digging graves brings in a bit more. When the families of the deceased come for funerals or to pay respects to the dead, they often leave a token, an "appreciation" as the young men put it, for looking after the cemetery and standing watch over the graves. One of the larger plots in the cemetery belongs to the Honorable Mr. Kaydea. His cement tomb is surrounded by a high wall topped with broken glass, creating a relatively secure place for the cemetery's living residents to stash their possessions and to sleep at night. Mr.

In the Duport Road Cemetery #1

Kaydea's son, the fighters claim, is a U.S. marine. When he comes to Liberia, they say, he is always generous and appreciative of the hard work these boys do looking after his father's resting place.

The Duport Road Cemetery is a gap, in the street parlance of Monrovia's ex-combatant populace. Congo Town Back Road, Zimbabwe, Titanic, the Ministry of Defense, the trash dump across UN Drive from the Truck Inn, and the beach at West Point are all gaps in the city.

The gap is a youth space, and often a violent one. It is not exclusively male but overwhelmingly masculine in its banter and its bravado. Gaps include the ghettoes of Monrovia, as the huts, houses, and street corners on which young men gather to drink, listen to music, and smoke are known. But the gap is more expansive. It encompasses the spaces and activities that radiate from the ghetto, a space of gathering and of living. It is in these spaces that ex-combatants accumulate, from which they are recruited and from which they operate, and between which they move.

On some level the Duport Road Cemetery and ex-combatants' other gaps are recognizable in the literature on interstitial spaces of the city and the possibilities such spaces represent today. The most famous of these, and perhaps the most widely employed, is Michel Foucault's heterotopias—a conceptualization of urban space that Foucault himself left vague.[5] In a 1967 lecture on architecture (Foucault 1986), a reference often employed by theorists of space, heterotopias were the spaces that exist between the formal, sanctioned spaces of the city. Heterotopias inverted or suspended the codes and behaviors that marked the normal as normal. Heterotopias allowed for those activities that could not be condoned or understood in the legitimate and lawful city, but upon which the city as a whole depended. It was in the heterotopia that the necessary experimentation and evolution of the city took place. Foucault lists a number of examples: brothels, colonies, boats, cemeteries, barracks, and prisons among them. Owing to their physical form, their intended uses, their extraneousness, or their association with waste and the abject, these spaces hosted activities and imaginings that were necessary but unthinkable or un-permitted elsewhere. It was, at least for Foucault, in its heterotopias that an urban populace could find new ways to inhabit the city.

David Harvey, in a critical review of the concept, therefore summarizes the appeal of the heterotopia idea not only for theorists but also for designers, planners, artists, and activists: "It [the heterotopia] enables us to look upon the multiple forms of deviant and transgressive behaviours and politics that occur in urban spaces . . . as valid and potentially meaningful reassertion to some kind of right to shape parts of the city in a different image" (2000: 184).

This basic idea, if not necessarily Foucault's terminology, has appeared across urban studies as a hopeful line of flight from the tightly regulated spaces of neoliberal commerce and restrictive citizenship that progressive commentators see dominating cities today. Tempered somewhat, it was, for example, an influence on the geographer Edward Soja's (1996) *Thirdspace*. Queer theorists have used the term to understand how otherwise restricted sexualities become visible in certain city spaces (see, for example, Allweil and Kallus [2008] on Tel Aviv's Independence Park), and others have seen the liminal spaces of immigrant housing and transit as heterotopias (see, for example, Olga 2013). Partha Chatterjee's (2004) "politics of the governed," in which most of the world's urban populace engages in politics not by formal participation in civil society but through creative negotiation with governing entities, presumes a heterotopic place-based politics.[6] Urban theorist David Grahame Shane (2005) disaggregates heterotopias into typologies with vary-ing degrees of planning and regulation, but argues (as in Foucault) that they are the only real spaces of urban possibility and invention outside the domi-nant codes of the city.[7] Proponents of radical architecture like Gil M. Doron go further. Every city contains erroneously labeled "dead zones" (Doron 2000, 2007). They are the by-products of the hegemonic forces that drive life in the modern city (notably the forces of modern capitalism). But they are spaces largely invisible to those same forces and into which official regulatory regimes generally don't reach. Within these spaces it is possible to find what Doron has called a (heterotopic) "transgressive architecture."[8]

At the center of much of this thinking is the presumption that the relative invisibility of certain spaces in the modern city affords a kind of protection. Those who dwell there are free to invent because, while they are in constant dialogue with the city writ large, they can tinker with its codes and conventions. They can explore new ways to make demands on other spaces and other actors in the city. Then, having fashioned new tools and developed new tactics, they can write new rules of engagement with those in power, at least to a point. A certain invisibility in the modern city creates spaces of new possibilities.

Implicitly or explicitly, at the heart of each of these heterotopic imaginaries is the threat of violence. In Chatterjee's politics of the governed it is the possibility of violent resistance that ultimately leads entities of power to negotiate with otherwise impotent communities. Similarly, there is an element of threat and insecurity in each of Doron's dead zones, a palpable precondition to creating the space of possibility outside the space of the normal.

Some version of the heterotopia would be a tempting analytic framework through which to understand the Duport Road Cemetery, as well as the many other spaces occupied by ex-combatants across Monrovia. There does indeed seem to be something transgressive in the inventive practices of Duport Road Cemetery's youth or the role-playing thefts outside the Truck Inn in Zimbabwe. There does seem something "agonistic and radically democratic" (Doron 2007) in the way ex-combatants sever and play with the logic of the city's social and political codes; in their threat of violence as the cost of ignoring their collective demands; in their practices of sharing and communalism; in the way they make urban detritus productive. Ex-combatants have enough of a sense of themselves as a category of populace (youth, rebel, ex-combatant) to have the "moral attributes of a community," one of Chatterjee's (2004: 57) crucial components for turning a population group into a "political society."

But reading Duport Road Cemetery or any of the other spaces inhabited

In the Duport Road Cemetery #2

by Monrovia's ex-combatants as heterotopias, transgressive architectures, or even as sites for enacting a politics of the governed would be a misreading. It would presume a relationship to these postwar city spaces and a political imaginary that simply is not there. It would be to mistake hypermobility for invisibility. It would misconstrue the threat of violence for a political project.

The fact is that spaces like the Duport Road Cemetery do not undo the dominant codes of the city. The youths who inhabit Monrovians' gap spaces often make claims on urban space, acts of seizure that are, as Chatterjee (2004: 75) puts it, the most frequent and important terrain of politics in the modern city. But there is in their claims no discernible "redefinition of property and the law" that could reasonably lead them to be called "political society" or that could mark the spaces they inhabit as the grounds from which such a political society could form. Instead, as I take up below, Monrovia's ex-combatants take those dominant codes to their logical extremes. Duport Road Cemetery is productive space, as is Zimbabwe, the Ministry of Defense, the E. J. Roye building, and even the small cubicle in which Human Garbage shelters. These are spaces of invention, experimentation, and serious play. But they are not heterotopic in the Foucauldian sense or any of its derivatives. These forms of invention are circumscribed for the most part by a very limited political imagination and a very narrow set of material possibilities.

Duport Road Cemetery is not a platform for political city making. It is only a space of urban subjection.

Placeless States and Stateless Places

I asked one of the men at Duport Road Cemetery how the ex-combatants who squatted there could stand to live among the dead, imagining that the powerful, invisible occult forces that impact these young men's lives in many ways must also figure in their relationship to the cemetery as a space of habitation. The dead, he responded matter-of-factly, don't live there anymore. Now it is only a space for the living. "In Monrovia," he added, "once you die, you're finished."

The question "Who does space belong to?" helps to illuminate the aporia between urban spaces that host seemingly unlimited possibilities for invention and experimentation, and the stunted political imaginaries simultaneously produced within those spaces. Nowhere is the contradiction more evident than in the swamplands of Monrovia's Congo Town and the sprawling settlement known as Peace Island.

When the Johnson Sirleaf government evicted the majority of ex-combatant squatters from the Ministry of Defense building, most ended up only a stone's throw away in an inhospitable bit of swamp called Peace Island. Peace Island is a place of uncertain ownership. There are rumors that the land belongs to the government, to a private family, to an unspecified American corporation, and to the military. There is also a remarkable diversity of stories about what, precisely, has been planned for Peace Island over the years. President William Tolbert (1971–1980), according to some, had set the land aside as an ethnic enclave for up-country Liberians coming to the city. Charles Taylor alternately promised it to an American company for unknown purposes or offered it as a barracks site for his army and militias. Ellen Johnson Sirleaf, it is rumored, intends to give the island to private investors for whatever uses they can put a malarial oasis to in the swamp. Most recently a Chinese proposal to level the old Ministry of Defense and build a massive new ministerial compound would allegedly extend well into the swamp, erasing much of Peace Island's current footprint.

But by all accounts, Peace Island was until recently a barren spit of land at the edge of Monrovia, inaccessible by foot or car during the rainy season when the waters of the river and the swamp ran high. "It was a forest," as one older resident of Peace Island, a former soldier, put it. "There were monkeys.

A lot of monkeys. The place was wild. It's a swamp!" Now Peace Island is a small town within the city, and it grows larger every day. One of the only published statistics on the number of Peace Island residents puts the population at 30,000, though it is not a number in which anyone has much faith (Williams 2011: 24).

Like everyone on Peace Island, the ex-combatant squatters evicted from the Ministry of Defense know that they will soon be evicted again. Despite the uncertainties around its ownership, despite the confusion over what is to be done with it, despite its general inhospitability and unsuitability for building and habitation, everyone on the island seems to know they are only temporary residents, though from past experience they also know that temporary can last a long time indeed.

However, even given the tangible sense that they are only in transit on Peace Island, almost as soon as they arrived there the ministry's ex-combatants began to build houses with the most durable material they could afford. Unlike the stereotype of informal urban settlements, Peace Island's inhabitants are not building tightly packed, makeshift compounds out of easily accessible materials. On Peace Island the houses of ex-combatants are freestanding, single structures surrounded by bare earth. Though they build them as quickly as possible, they do so with the most solid materials they can afford, even if this means that their houses are uninhabitable for long periods while the necessary materials are collected.

None of this would seem to make sense given the precarious and temporary claim that Peace Island's residents actually have to the island. Why is there such a mad rush to build permanent housing on a temporary landscape? Why invest so much precious capital and sweat equity in a house that will soon be torn down? Why maintain an already-ruined-but-as-yet-unbuilt structure? This is not, after all, the story of these combatants' wartime experience, in which the instability and liquidity of barracks spaces was part of what made them effective vehicles from which to make claims on the city. It is also not the dominant mode of architecture in the city, where historically uncertain ownership laws make even successful businesses hesitant to entrench themselves too firmly through permanent infrastructure (see introduction). And it would seem to run counter to the animating spirit of movement and omnilocality that otherwise propels young men around and around Monrovia.

And yet the logics are hardly contradictory at all. The story that Peace

Island's inhabitants tell is that when the time comes to move them out, the government will have no choice but to compensate them for "their" land and the structures they have erected on it. There are too many trained military personnel on Peace Island for the government to evict them by force. So agents of the government will be deployed, when the time comes, to value the structures on the island and compensate their inhabitants accordingly. "I have hope," said one young ex-soldier: "I am a citizen of this country. I have a free mind. This is a decent area. So we pray [that the government will not try to evict us by force]. That government will feel for us, because we are citizens. If any NGO or government says we must go, then maybe they will see the value of my house, and they will help us to go. If they see the house and it's a fine, fine house, and they satisfy me, then I will go. I am citizen of the country!"

The compensation for one's labors, he says, will be entirely dependent on one's physical presence on the urban landscape and the work one has done to fix that space through material, built forms. The rights that stem from being a "citizen of the country" are inextricably bound to being (temporarily) fixed in space, visible through the "fine, fine house" that one has managed to establish on otherwise unclaimed or ambiguous territory. "He thinks he can put down a foundation and the government will compensate him because he is a citizen," was how one ex-combatant described the thinking of the average Peace Island resident. The larger and more solid one's footprint, the greater one's claim to citizenship, understood here again as the right to compensation for one's work. In every way, cement block is more solid than mud brick; mud brick is preferable to zinc; zinc is stronger than wood—though one has to make do with what one has.

These squatters' rights are not guaranteed in Liberian law. Liberia's legal code is a jumbled mess when it comes to the rights of occupation. By custom, squatters have been allowed to stay provided there is no recognized land-owner who complains. No law guarantees that those dislocated by postwar development projects will be compensated, and different government agencies have different practices in this regard, often depending on the sources of development funding and the requirements of donors.

In this regard, Peace Island's former life as an uninhabited swampland of uncertain destiny is an important part of its mythology. A "dark forest filled with monkeys" is, as another resident put it, "neutral ground. It doesn't belong to anyone." Until, of course, someone claims it, and makes that claim visible in a tangible, material way. At that point it becomes, literally and figuratively, the grounds on which to stake claims to the rights to the city. It is the logic that Njami has argued lies at the heart of African urbanism: the truly African part of the urban fabric is the "no man's land where the space seems to belong to the person occupying it, and to him alone" (2001: 79).

Take the odd little enclave known as V.P. Grave. Enoch Dogolea was Charles Taylor's vice president until 2000, when he died, either of natural causes or at the hands of Taylor himself, depending on whose version of Liberia's recent history one subscribes to. A small group of former Taylor men now sleep atop the marble mausoleum that holds Dogolea's body behind a church outside the Red Light neighborhood of Monrovia. The area was a Taylor stronghold for years, and a more or less watertight zinc canopy covers the gravesite.

V.P. Grave makes a spare but dry pavilion for a group of men who sell drugs during the day and run an armed robbery operation at night. "This is our base," one of them said as we sat next to Dogolea's final resting place. "We can go anywhere, but this is our base. It's a free area. No one owns it. It's government land. We decided to settle on government land because government lied to us." One of the young men then volunteered that the vice president of a country should be treated with more respect. His grave deserved security, and so these young men have appointed themselves to provide it. Now, having inserted themselves into the otherwise unoccupied site, the government should recognize (and compensate) them as that security presence.

Peace Island and V.P. Grave, like Duport Road Cemetery, are blank spaces in which ex-combatants are free to invent. But they are not sites that can be occupied differently. Their logics of ownership and occupation are creative but not transformative. They articulate no right to the city. The men who inhabit those spaces know that their physical presence is potentially valuable only through the variable of violence and only if and when they are forced to move again. Unlike the agents of "venture capital" that Rao (2007) sees inserting themselves into the ruin spaces of the city in order to imagine a postwar future, the ex-combatants in Monrovia's gaps only see themselves suspended in ambiguous space, waiting for the financial rewards of forced mobility through a fragmented landscape. Here young men seem free to invent new forms, but not to reinvent or even reimagine the flows and logics of Monrovia's urban grid.[9]

"If any NGO or government says we must go . . . they will help us to go."
There is in that claim a second telling ambiguity. The state to which postwar
youth can appeal is impossible to locate. It may be a government agency,
though it could as easily be a foreign government like the United States, or
the United Nations, an NGO, or the World Bank. The point is that this man,
like thousands of others, sees himself surrounded by a diverse landscape of
authorizing institutions. Any one of these may make a claim on the space he
occupies, and so his labor is to make himself as materially fixed in that location as he possibly can without being bound to that space or dependent upon
it in any substantial way—over and over in spaces across the city.

Here again the placelessness of both the ex-combatant populace and the
state itself distinguishes the practice of politics in much of post–Cold War
West Africa from what Chatterjee (2004) has argued is the prevailing mode
of politics in cities across much of the world. Even with the relative stability of
the Johnson Sirleaf government, for most Monrovians the Liberian state remains largely a "simulacral regime" (Mbembe 1992; see also Piot 2010: 2–12).
It is hard, sometimes impossible, to know how or to whom to direct one's
demands when the state governs primarily through spectacle and hollow,
inconsistent performances. The kinds of politics through negotiation and ac-
commodation that might succeed in the Indian context are rendered virtually
unthinkable when the state or city government is widely understood to be
existent but largely vacant.

On the opposite side of Monrovia from Peace Island, the ruins of the Liberia Broadcasting System (LBS) building stand like a fortress at the crest of
a steep hill. The LBS was designed and built by the same Israeli firm that constructed the Ministry of Defense, and its exterior design is almost identical—
brutalist, concrete modernism with an impregnable, martial air. Also like
the Ministry of Defense, it was never finished. For over fifteen years its only
occupants have been squatters (see chapter 4).

In early 2012, those residents had not yet relocated, but they were well
aware that their tenure inside LBS was likely to be short. Martin, the young
man who served as deputy chairman of the LBS residents' association, described a recent meeting with the head of the broadcasting service. The LBS
had no plans ever to move into the badly damaged building, but it did hope to
sell the structure in the near future. (As with many of these structures, there
is no buyer more specific than "a private company," most likely an American

or, increasingly, a Chinese one.) Some eighty families were living in the LBS, according to Martin, all originally from outside Monrovia. All of them, he argued, wanted to go home. Monrovia was too expensive, too dangerous, and too alien for them to make their lives there, despite the fact that they had done so for more than a decade. The majority of those years were postwar years in which the residents of LBS did not necessarily need the security of the city as they did when they first fled the fighting in the countryside. And yet they stayed on. The reason, according to Martin, was that no one would leave without compensation. "We will not just gather our things and walk out," he told me. "We are asking the owners of this building to compensate us." But this was, as Martin framed it and as so many others implied, not compensation for a future denied, or for the opportunities that young men had imagined and invented for themselves by working invisibly at the urban margins. They would do nothing to resist being forced out because in truth they had no desire to stay. The only thing that these young men were able to invent in the gaps of Monrovia were new strategies of mobility, new ways to flow through the city profitably. What they sought were the profits of a canny market calculus, the benefits of being in the way.

Living Dangerously

A. B., himself an ex-fighter with LURD, was particularly excited to have met Human Garbage in person. Human Garbage was indeed well known in Monrovia, and even now his picture is for sale in the market as part of a collage of wartime images with which one can, if one chooses, wallpaper one's walls. For days after we met him, A. B. asked what I thought of Human Garbage, and he told the story over and over again of how Human Garbage tried to fool us into thinking he remained a man of substance. Like the young men at Congo Town Back Road, A. B. seemed to find Human Garbage's current situation immensely funny. But even as he mocked him, there was a certain wariness. A. B. told the story less as a joke than as a parable. There was a spark of recognition in the way he recounted the details. He seemed to find it amusing not because Human Garbage had attempted to bluff his way into legibility but because, despite his fearsome reputation as a man who had achieved things in the past, his performance that day was so inept.

It is a scenario played out daily in Monrovia just as it plays out in cities across the continent. Monrovia today looks very much like those cities described by writers like Simone, de Boeck, and Njami: a liquid, immaterial city, a heterotopic space of invention. It is a form of African urbanism, moreover, that would seem to reflect all the potential that Chatterjee and other observers see in interstitial urban spaces for the creation of a political society. Elsewhere at this same historical moment, a global landscape of urban political movements is doing just that, what Harvey (2012) has called "a spirit of protest and revolt [that] spread contagiously through urban networks." And this is a landscape of which Monrovians are well aware. The so-called Arab Spring, globally circulating Occupy movements, and other land-based political movements were the topic of conversation in Monrovia as they were around the globe at the start of the millennium's second decade. Add to this Monrovia's long history of violence and a continued discourse of violent mobilization. Liberia's ex-combatants resort continuously to the language of renewed warfare and a new revolution if their situation does not improve. Monrovia would seem a city in which the most radical, even militant, practices of new urban living would be reproduced and expanded upon.

What one does not find among Monrovia's ex-combatant squatters, however, is any kind of political imaginary that allows these elements to congeal into a political society. For all its inventiveness, Monrovia's ex-combatants have yet to invent a new politics of space or a new politics of urban life. They make little effort to stake a claim on those elements of the built environment that they do occupy outside of the claim that it has a market value when it is taken from them. They have not yet invented a politics of the governed that would lead them to mount a serious protest or offer coordinated resistance when they are evicted from buildings like the Ministry of Defense, urban spaces in which they have lived for more than a decade, and after which they are forced to dwell in even more inhospitable and untenable gaps in the city. Indeed, such evictions are not only inevitable but perversely desirable because they may be profitable, though that is not guaranteed.

The upshot is that for most of Monrovia's ex-combatants, the city exists only partially "beyond its architecture" (de Boeck 2011). It might be more fitting to describe a populace that cannot imagine that the city's architecture can have a different meaning. Young men inhabit the city's ruin spaces as just that: ruin spaces. These spaces are, moreover, nodes in a network of such ruins through which they quickly cycle, entrenching themselves temporarily when that seems the most effective strategy for making movement possible and profitable again. For all the insecurity and uncertainty they face living such a precarious existence, Monrovia's ex-combatants have not yet learned to live dangerously enough.

THE LIMITS TO INVENTION within Monrovia's gaps, the limits that kept gap spaces from becoming heterotopias and its ex-combatants from becoming a political community, were set by a host of factors. Among these was the very shape and form of the city itself, or at least those gaps within it that made up ex-combatants' circuits of movement. Understanding those limits means taking seriously the built environment of the city as architecture—as, in other words, politically ordering forms. That is my project in the next four chapters.

CHAPTER 2

The Ministry of Defense
Excessive Architecture

MINISTRY of
DEFENSE
FROM PEACE ISLAND

Field sketch, Ministry of Defense

I t surprised no one when the fighters who occupied the Ministry of Defense were told to leave. What was surprising was how little the ministry's occupants resisted their eviction.

The building's inhabitants had established themselves in the vast expanses of the structure. Partitions of varying degrees of solidity marked out rooms and common spaces. Plastic, metal, and bamboo walls created a complex series of internal enclosures that domesticated the otherwise cavernous open floor plan. Petty traders worked the corridors and set up small shops. A taxi rank had been established on the ministry grounds to facilitate the movement of the building's residents to other parts of the city. This was not a casual occupation, and many of the soldiers and ex-combatants who lived there were firmly entrenched.

Most had few other options for housing in the city. Those forced to leave the ministry could not easily be absorbed by the existing urban housing stock, even within its large informal settlements. Ex-combatants removed from spaces like this faced a future with only the roughest of temporary shelter.

But when told to go, the men at the ministry did not put up a fight. "It's the government's building," said one former resident, a young man now living in the swamp of Peace Island. "They can do whatever they want with it." It was a common sentiment, repeated again and again by its former occupants. The building belonged to the government, and the state's reclamation of it was

Ministry of Defense #1

Ministry of Defense #2

Ministry of Defense #3

Ministry of Defense #5

FACING PAGE: *Ministry of Defense #4*

Ministry of Defense #6

Ministry of Defense #7

Ministry of Defense #8

FACING PAGE: *Ministry of Defense #9*

Ministry of Defense #10

London Occupy, 2013. In cities across the world, the end of the first decade of the millennium was marked by protests over rights to the city.

neither extraordinary nor unwarranted. "Government needed that building," another young man added, "and so we just had to abide by it because that is development." "[They moved us out so that] by and by some good can come out of it," said a third. The one thing I never heard from the ministry's evicted *wow!!!* residents was that they had any right to remain there.

When the time came, these men, men with a long history of taking up arms and who faced a very bleak future, refused to stake a claim on the space in which they had made their lives. Why did they put up no resistance to this forced mobility, when they would seem to have had both the tools and the motivation to do so?

It is an even more baffling question when one considers that their eviction took place against the backdrop of a global landscape of urban resistance movements, a "spirit of protest and revolt [that] spread contagiously through urban networks" (Harvey 2012: 116). Although local in their demands, residents of cities across the Americas, Europe, and Asia at the same time were claiming new rights to the city by occupying urban spaces and refusing to leave (see Holston 2008; Hou 2010; Juris 2012; Juris and Razsa 2012).

Contemporaneously, across North Africa long-term occupations of public space resulted in the downfall of governments. Protests at Tahrir Square in

Cairo and in plazas in cities across Tunisia seemed to signal an era of popular protest politics through the highly visible seizure of public and government spaces. The civil war that eventually led to the overthrow of Muammar Gaddafi in Libya had its origins in, among other events, popular protests against housing shortages in multiple Libyan cities.

While Occupy movements and mass demonstrations were not widespread in West African cities, the logic of spectacular occupation has been part of urban politics in this region for some time. In Lomé, for example, Togolese squatted in the park opposite the U.S. embassy as a way to assert their right to apply for a U.S. diversity visa (Piot 2012). The popular youth-led Y'en a Marre and M23 mobilizations against Senegalese president Abdoulaye Wade included mass demonstrations in Dakar's Place de l'Obélisque, along with forms of virtual organizing through popular music and social networking media.

Monrovians are no less adept than other urbanites at this kind of popular politics. At the height of the siege of Monrovia in 2003, the city's residents piled dead bodies in front of the U.S. embassy, using corpses to claim a right to urban security by appropriating a space reserved for power. Monrovia's newspapers have been filled for years with stories of street protests related to corruption, wages, or political party infighting. And Monrovians were no less aware than Caraqueños, Nicosians, or San Franciscans that residents of other cities were using their bodies and grassroots organizing to make counterclaims to the rights to the city—including, in many cases, the right to create spaces of shelter in the city's abandoned or ruined infrastructure.

And yet against this background, and in this most seemingly obvious of circumstances, the residents of the Ministry of Defense did little or nothing to resist their forced removal. Largely without protest, they left. Why?

As Filip de Boeck (2013) notes, it is very difficult to imagine an Arab Spring–like uprising in most sub-Saharan African cities. The logics of space are too fragmented and shifting, the sense of a common identity and destiny too ephemeral and unstable. What is more, as I argued in chapter 1, there is at the moment a sense among Monrovia's ex-combatants that mobility itself is productive. It can be strategic to be fixed in space temporarily, even to give the appearance of permanence, but movement is the real locus of profit. At least for young men, to live and to labor is to move.

But these explanations are not exhaustive. They do not completely account for why, set against the backdrop of incredible need and a global assemblage of images of urban resistance, the population of the Ministry of Defense simply left when they were told to go.

The ruins of the Ministry of Defense building itself suggest another piece in the puzzle of why popular political mobilizations sometimes fail to emerge: some aspects of the built environment refuse to be imagined as spaces of popular politics. Some urban forms work against a population group becoming a "political society," in Chatterjee's (2004) terms. It is possible, as a matter of design, history, or both, for certain forms to be so saturated with meaning that they actively resist being imagined otherwise. Slavoj Žižek (1997: 3–4) has argued that the contradictions and fictions of a political ideology can be read in the architecture that it inspires. But the corollary is that, contradictory though it may be, some architectures express that ideology so completely that they can be impossible to reinterpret or resist.

The Ministry of Defense is a striking case example. It is an unmistakably brutalist building. That term is most often used to describe, or decry, any monumental concrete structure. In the popular imaginary of architecture, it evokes images of Soviet-bloc totalitarian aesthetics (Abrahamson 2011). It has been applied to Louis Kahn's Yale University Art Center and Paul Rudolph's Art and Architecture Building; Boston City Hall; the J. Edgar Hoover Building in Washington, DC; and to any number of postcolonial projects in Africa, Latin America, and the former Soviet Union. Yet brutalism, or more accurately the new brutalism, has a more specific, nuanced, and progressive history. Evaluating the Ministry of Defense as built form, and understanding its architectural history, suggests that there are real limits to how far urban residents can go in experimenting and inventing within the built environment that surrounds them. There are, in other words, limits to how much they can live beyond their architecture.

The New Brutalism

The philosopher Gilles Deleuze (1989) argued in a book on postwar cinema that the devastation of European cities in the 1940s led a small cadre of artists to new visions of what it meant to see and inhabit modern urban space. This was, Deleuze argued, a literal revisioning. Learning to live in the postwar city meant learning to see the city differently and to see different possibilities within the city.

Within architecture, brutalism was part of that new urban vision. The architects most strongly associated with the new brutalism are the British designers Alison and Peter Smithson. Though they built surprisingly little, their extensive body of writing and paper architecture had an outsized influence on the development of modern design from the 1950s well into the 1980s, and a disproportionate impact on African architecture in particular.

The Smithsons began their interventions in modern architecture with a radical vision for devastated postwar London. The English architectural establishment's program for rebuilding British cities was a relatively conservative contemporary aesthetic. Postwar housing and development projects were seen as opportunities to find and reclaim a distinctly English building style, something that would restore to the nation its pride and sense of identity (Banham [1955] 2011: 20–21, 1966; Curtis 1996: 529; Gold 1997).

For the Smithsons and their cohort of young architects, this was a betrayal of both the progressive politics and the internationalism of early modern masters like Le Corbusier and Mies van der Rohe (Banham [1955] 2011: 15–18, 1966; Crosby [1955] 2011: 17–18; Kitnick 2011: 4; Smithson 2001: 41). Their response was a severe design program that they considered an ethical rather than aesthetic project (Smithson and Smithson [1957] 2011: 241). Architecture should not be a tool for rebuilding the state. It was an opportunity to retool postwar subjectivity for the modern world. The world was changing radically, and architecture was a heroic enterprise that would allow the dispirited postwar working classes in particular to find and express their own heroism. "Brutalism tries to face up to a mass-produced society," they famously wrote, and "drag a rough poetry out of the confused and powerful forces which are at work" (Smithson and Smithson [1957] 2011: 37). In his commentaries on the Hunstanton School, one of their first and most famous works, Peter Smithson was even more hyperbolic: "It is through BUILT FORM that the inherent nobility of man finds release" (Smithson 2001: 42, emphasis in original).

In an extensive analysis of what this meant in practice, Reyner Banham ([1955] 2011) describes an architecture based on the idea that a building's layout should be immediately clear ("formal legibility of plan"); that its physical support structures should be obvious ("clear exhibition of structure"); and that its materials should be undecorated ("valuation of materials for their inherent qualities 'as found'"). This tripartite definition of brutalism was a consequence of the Marxian understanding of class division that circulated among the Smithsons' artistic circles. Freedom for the working classes needed to begin with truth telling and dismantling Marx's "camera obscura of ideology," the masking of the real conditions that made it impossible for workers to perceive the causes of their exploitation. Formal symmetry and the undisguised exhibition of structure and material were part of a larger project of peeling back all manner of dishonesty. Modernist architecture as a machine for the production of images is a theme that has run through much of the critical literature (see, for example, Cohen 2012; Forty 2012; Mostafavi and Leatherbarrow 1993: 91–92; Zimmerman 2004). But in brutalism, with its emphasis on the potential in both form and material to communicate political messages, the logic of the image is particularly dominating. And it lies at the heart of brutalism's global appeal.

The new brutalist sensibility was deeply impacted by the emerging logic of mass advertising in 1950s Europe and the United States (Banham 1966: 62–67; see also Gold 1997: 224). Like television advertising, the Smithsons intended architecture to be a communicative medium for imparting instantly apprehensible, affective images. Affecting images need not be images of beauty, and indeed for the brutalists they rarely were. Instead the form of the building taken as a whole should elicit a profound response. As Gerhard Kallmann, one of the principal architects of the Boston City Hall and a self-described brutalist put it, "It [Boston City Hall] had to be awesome, not just pleasant and slick" (Havesit 2012). While any architecture presumably aspires to be emotionally affecting, the brutalist structure was intended to immediately express a lasting (visual) concept. Like 1950s television advertising, nothing about that message should be subtle or hidden. Inside and out, brutalist structures were meant to make visible the raw essence of their materials in a single, consistent visual statement, a statement selling a single idea. It is an architecture of "surfaces" (see Leatherbarrow and Mostafavi 2002; Kitnick 2011: 4), meaning an architecture that leaves little space for ambiguous or indeterminate experiences. Brutalist architecture should intervene in the everyday worlds of those who come into contact with it by clearly broadcasting an unmistakable message.

Perhaps not surprisingly, it was largely in the service of the state that the network of architects and designers in dialogue with the Smithsons carried the brutalist aesthetic outside Britain, most notably to cities in the colonial and early postcolonial Global South.[1] Two other British architects, Maxwell

Fry and Jane Drew, and the tropical architecture movement they helped to develop, forged a direct connection between postwar British architecture and the development of urban forms in late colonial and early postcolonial Africa. Fry and Drew were originally posted in Britain's West African colonies in the mid-1940s as urban planners and subsequently opened an independent architecture practice that completed public projects in Ghana, Nigeria, and Togo, notably museums and school campuses (Hess 2000; Liscombe 2006). As educators in the influential tropical architecture section of the Architecture Association in London, Fry and Drew had significant impact on both the actual built forms of government projects in West Africa and on the thinking of architects who came after them (see Fry and Drew 1956; as well as Chalfin 2014; le Roux 2003; le Roux and Uduku 2004; Uduku 2006).

For Fry and Drew, no less than for the Smithsons, what was to be advertised in the new architecture were new possibilities for urban life. Built form would mediate the relationship between emergent technologies and urban living, largely through its capacity to advertise new ways of being. "Modern architecture, and its extension into town planning," they wrote in a manual on tropical building, should create "unities of unresolved thought and feeling in the form of buildings, groups of buildings and larger aggregations in which life may know its bounds and flourish" (Fry and Drew 1956: 20; cited also in Liscombe 2006: 204).

The project of letting life "flourish" through architecture was considerably easier in colonial and postcolonial Africa than in Britain. With little regulation or oversight, less competition, and access to cheap labor, modern architects were more free to experiment in Africa than elsewhere (see Gogan and Rowley 2011; see also Fuller 2007; Wright 1991). For most it was an article of faith that the experiments in new architecture could be a catalyst for social transformation despite differing cultural assumptions and nationalist goals in various West African countries (see Liscombe 2006: 195).

The brutalist buildings appearing in West Africa were, then, intended to be powerful communicative statements. And as the client for most of these projects was the state itself, it is hardly surprising that state power became inextricably linked to the power of architecture to, in Peter Smithson's phrase, release "the inherent nobility of man." Brutalism's philosophical underpinnings fit with the ethos of nation building and modernization sweeping Africa, and its muscularity and heavy-handedness mirrored the drive of African elites to consolidate and advertise state authority. What began as a politically progressive, avant-garde architectural movement in postwar European housing quickly spread outward to become a major component in what Brian Larkin has described as the complex function of modern infrastructure in Africa. While it bequeaths modernity on African cities, it does so within highly prescribed limits and at the cost of uncompromising and unsparing political subjection (Larkin 2008: 245).

Excessive Architecture

It was not only in West Africa that brutalism found a ready group of adherents. In Israel, the *sabra* (Israeli-born) architects coming of age in the 1950s saw in brutalism an aesthetic more fitting than classical modernism for creating a unified Israeli Jewish identity (Nitzan-Shiftan 2010: 90–92). By the 1980s, brutalism had therefore become part of the standard vocabulary of Israeli architecture (Nitzan-Shiftan 2007).

The complex provenance of Monrovia's Ministry of Defense makes this an important element in the building's story. YONA International was a multinational conglomerate referred to in the Liberian press as an Israeli corporation with interests in logging and large-scale construction. YONA was one of a number of private commercial channels through which U.S. and Israeli support for Liberia during the Cold War could flow. According to T. Dempster Brown, a Monrovia lawyer who sued the government in late 2012 over plans to demolish the building, YONA was paid more than U.S. $25 million by the Doe government to construct its new defense headquarters (see "Liberia: GoL Sued" 2012). Another 2012 press story describes a financing deal in which YONA was allowed to construct the ministry as a scheme to avoid paying Liberian taxes on its logging interests. A third version suggests that one of the largest timber concessions in West Africa was given to a YONA partner corporation as payment for constructing the ministry, a building that the Doe government wanted but could not afford. Further complicating matters, according to the army chief of staff at the time, the land on which the ministry sits was purchased from the Tolbert family; Samuel Doe became president of Liberia by overthrowing William Tolbert only a few years before (see Karmo 2012).

When Samuel Doe contracted to have the ministry built, what he sought was the advertising potential inherent in the building. Doe needed an architecture that would immediately confirm a simple but contestable message: that his soldiers had, through force of arms, seized the state and that they had the strength to keep it. This was in no way a building for the Liberian people. The Ministry of Defense was about militarized state authority. It advertised the martial strength of the Liberian state under the direction of a young soldier. Smithson-style brutalism may have begun as a progressive ethical response to the housing needs of a devastated city, but in African and Israeli cities, it endures as a machine for the production of state authority. Unlike the Smithsons' heroic vision of the unfettered worker of the future, in Monrovia the image that brutalist architecture broadcast was a picture of heroic armed power.

What are the consequences of an architecture so saturated with the message of state? All architecture is communicative. But what of architecture whose sole message is that of the power and authority of martial sovereignty? Given that militarized state authority is the singular guiding principle of the Ministry of Defense, its strongest analogies are not the architecture of other postcolonial ministry buildings, even those in cities such as Chandigarh, Brasília, Dodoma, or Abuja that adhere to modern movement principles. A closer built analog is, rather, the tectonic logic in the total control architecture of the postmodern prison.

Evolving practices of containment, like the U.S. military detention center at Guantanamo Bay, Cuba, and the rapid expansion of immigrant holding facilities around the world, pose a challenge to the Foucauldian analysis of the prison as a disciplinary institution. Judith Butler (2004), for example, has argued that in Guantanamo there is no subject at all: that this is a facility designed exclusively for the management of bare life as an act of sovereignty.[2] Unlike Bentham's panopticon, these prison spaces do not create subjects who regulate themselves. Instead Butler and others argue that Guantanamo, and by extension other spaces in the world today, are zones of exception in which sovereign authority is exercised in naked forms. In Mbembe's (2003) terms, these are spaces of necropolitics, spaces in which the rights of authority are exercised by deciding how death, rather than life, should be managed. The goal of these spaces of exception, whether they are prisons, camps, detention centers, or other restricted zones, is not to rehabilitate prisoners, not to reform terrorists, not to evaluate or repatriate border crossers, not to produce workers or economic subjects. The goal is to solidify the authority of the sovereign through the management and, if necessary, extermination of bodies. It is impossible within such spaces to do much more than perform the limited tasks deemed acceptable by those in positions of power and to perform those tasks in tightly controlled and regulated ways.

Such zones of exception require a clear demarcation of space, and thus a particular architecture. To reach the point of non-subject-producing space requires an absurd design. It must render space unfamiliar. The architecture of the space of nonsubjectivity needs to relate to the process of life in ways that differ markedly from life outside. Space must become alien to such a degree that those forced into them simply cannot recognize how to live there in a familiar and meaningful way. Built forms are uninhabitable when, in Ian Buchanan and Gregg Lambert's phrase, "the modern subject no longer recognizes the space in which it is located" (2005: 6). This is excessive architecture.

In her book on supermax prisons in the United States, Lorna Rhodes (2004) describes spaces in which architecture becomes a totalizing tool for the movement and storage of bodies. Given the prisoner's perceived capacity to imagine new, weaponized uses for the mundane objects around him, the enclosing space must be rendered unrecognizable in any useful sense. All "complexities," as Rhodes puts it, are to "remain in the hands of management" (23). Windows through which no one can see, doors through which nothing can pass, platforms that are and are not beds, fixtures that are both sinks and toilets, lights that cannot be regulated, and featureless walls that contain everything. All of these elements create a world of total orchestration.

The result is not a space of discipline. Prisoners subject to this total confinement do not emerge as social beings. Their capacity to function as social creatures at all is, if anything, even further eroded. "The prison environment," Rhodes writes, "could not be better designed to activate a sense of threat to the coherence of the self" (56).

This postdisciplinary prison succeeds, if that is the correct term, because it creates an environment that is uninhabitable. It is non-subject-producing because those who are subject to it do not know how to live there. They can move through these spaces, even reside in them for extended periods. But they cannot dwell in them in any meaningful way. These are spaces that do not allow their inhabitants to imagine alternative futures. It is an architecture that works actively, if not always successfully, to mitigate the capacity for imagination and experimentation.

There is no question that the Ministry of Defense building is inhospitable. But to label it a brutalist building implies an excessiveness. It implies the rigid set of formal characteristics envisioned by the Smithsons and their cohort. But it also implies the violence of authoritarianism and urban subjugation, the possibility of becoming non-subject-producing, alien space. The ministry, given its raw concrete construction, its symmetry and legibility of plan, its sheer scale, and its unmistakable association with militarized state power, did both.

An Aesthetic of Images

In plan, the ministry is an almost perfect square. Identical octagonal turrets stand at each outside corner. A massive inner courtyard at the heart of the structure exaggerates the rigid geometry. Though the façade of the building are badly scarred (and in some cases incomplete), the intended design was clearly a repetitive pattern of windows set in shallow bays. A viewer would be able to immediately understand the layout of the structure, interior and exterior, from virtually any vantage point. Like all brutalist buildings, the Ministry of Defense would have no secrets and no internal hierarchy. These are structures that establish hierarchies outside themselves, in relation to the world around them.

The Ministry of Defense does so by making visibility a crucial part of the building's program. But it inverts the politics of vision. This is a building that reserves for itself the right to look. Set on a slight hill, it is impossible to view the building from anywhere except below it. There are no window openings of any kind below what would effectively be the second floor of the building. The most accessible windows would have been in the corner towers, and these are slit designs that closely resemble the archers' portals in a medieval European castle. Recessing the repetitive glazing on the façade de-emphasizes them as visual access points into the building, but exaggerates their eyelike function. They look out much more effectively than they look in. Consistent with brutalist image logic, the building is immediately visually graspable from any angle, but anyone within sight of the building is also powerfully aware of being simultaneously caught in the building's gaze.

Only two elements break the symmetry. Perversely, both underscore, rather than disrupt, the sense of an unassailable sovereign that stands apart from the people below. The first is a massive viewing stand on the top floor of the building. The sculptural stairs and benches are positioned to give a commanding view of the large open ground in front of the building, a perch over the parade ground from which Doe and his senior military officers could personally inspect their troops.

Here again the form and placement of this architectural feature would seem to work against it being understood, and appropriated, as anything other than an artifact of a state of emergency and the imposition of military authority. The steps and seating are outsized and inhumanly shaped. They seem deliberately distorted or caricatured, as though sculpted to accommodate what Mbembe (1992) once called the "vulgar" aesthetics of the African big man with his swollen body and grossly scaled appetites. The viewing stand is positioned so high above the earth that it establishes no relationship to the ground; it would be strikingly impractical and ineffective as a space for publicly dramatizing the connection between a military leader and his troops. The view from the stand is sweeping and imperial, but it creates no interface between exterior and interior. It offers only a god's-eye view of seemingly unlimited surveillance.

The second break in the symmetry of the ministry is an inexplicable protrusion from the front of the building. It is possible that the sculpted form was intended to support some elaborate porte cochère in the original building design. More likely, however, it was simply intended as a strong sculptural element, the sole decorative feature on an otherwise Spartan façade. Regardless of its intended use, however, the impact of the feature is much the same as with the viewing platform: it relates to something seemingly larger than human. Its scale is disproportionate to those who might occupy the space. As a result, it has none of the effect of mediating inside and outside at the building's entry. If it is proportionate to anything recognizable, it is to the superhuman persona cultivated by big-man rulers like Doe and, even more so, his successor Charles Taylor. Once again, this is an excessive architecture that renders even the most mundane of functions, entry and exit from a building, absurd.

This problem of scale runs throughout the building. The rooftop of the ministry was allegedly designed to offer multiple landing pads for the helicopters of the president and his chief ministers. The towers of the corner stairwells are massive fortifications rather than simple passageways. The interior courtyard is so dwarfed by the surrounding edifice that it feels more like a gladiatorial arena than an inner sanctum.

The building's outsized capacities are reflected in the way Monrovians discuss it. General Henry Dubar, the former chief of staff for the Liberian army, claimed improbably that the roof of the building was large enough to serve as a runway for planes. Interviewed by a Monrovia newspaper regarding his court case to prevent the building from being demolished, T. Dempster Brown described an enormous tunnel leading out from the basement that could allegedly serve to load huge caches of weaponry into submarines ("Liberia: GoL Sued" 2012). Hassan, a LURD fighter who had lived in the ministry a number of different times over the years, said simply, "It was a city by itself."

What this massive scale and symmetry does is confound the senses, making the usual techniques for giving meaning to architectural space impossible. As Walter Benjamin (1968) put it, architecture is made sensible by relating to its details in a "state of distraction," as those who inhabit a space pursue other projects and goals. A structure that appears as an immense totality and at inhuman scale, as does the Ministry of Defense, is a building in which it is challenging to be distracted by other activities.

In press accounts of the Ministry of Defense, the building is most often characterized as "bulletproof," a term that I heard Major Sandi and other ex-combatants use as well (see also Parley 2013). It is a telling metaphor. The structure seemed impregnable in virtually every sense. Its tectonics, architectural historian Kenneth Frampton's (1990) term for the poetics of construction, the union of the engineering and art required to make a building both stand up and mean something, seemed impervious to intervention—including those interventions of the squatters who attempted to domesticate the space with their own temporary architecture and design.

Like many large structures in the postcolonial tropics, the Ministry of Defense is made from rough concrete. Only the support columns are reinforced with steel. Otherwise most of the façade is simple concrete block infill, relatively thin, cheaply made, and assembled without forms or skilled labor. As a result, though both the structural members and the infill walls are concrete, they have a very different aesthetic. The structural, reinforced concrete pillars read as solid, supporting masses, whereas the small block infill reads as less substantial, even flimsy by comparison. In a completed building this difference between the two forms of concrete would most likely be masked (though doing so would not be orthodox new brutalism). Without that mask it is difficult to make the two elements cohere. The material support appears overwhelming in proportion to the materials that define the space, the more human, domestic side of the construction. In the ministry most of this infill is gone, leaving the muscular structural supports. Hence the need for residents to import their own building materials to carve up the massive space. As a result, the occupied space of the ministry consists of two kinds of material: a raw and permanent structure that holds the building up and the more ephemeral and bricolaged materials that divide its interior space. The way these materials meet one another is the building's tectonics, and there a significant part of its meaning as a human habitat lies.

Just as the plan of the ministry and its scale made it a structure that seemed to relate only to the sovereign power of the Liberian state, so too do the tectonics of the building challenge the idea that the space can be meaningfully appropriated and claimed by anyone operating with human material or at a merely human scale. The reinforced concrete columns of the building belong to a different tectonic order than the plastic sheeting, zinc, cardboard, and wood scraps out of which inhabitants could fashion their own infill walls, floors, and ceilings. There was no way to join these elements in a unified and meaningful synthesis. The building's bones, its basic structure, would always stand apart from anything the residents might do to it or within it. Their own efforts would always be provisional and transitory; those of the Liberian state would always have an aura of permanence.

It need not be this way. The bricolage, ad hoc aesthetics of colonized structures can develop their own logic of assembly and coherent, meaningful tectonic orders. The residents of the Torre David tower in Caracas, for example, used locally produced concrete blocks to subdivide the spaces of an unfinished forty-five-floor tower that was structurally very similar to the Ministry of Defense. But at Torre David an infill of concrete block used in concert with other more transitory materials like wood, zinc, and plastic became an architecture of permanence. In the barrios of Caracas, such ad hoc infill is part of the local building vocabulary; it is an architecture in its own right, made meaningful by the mass waves of urban migrants and by the Chavez regime's rhetoric of rights to the city for the urban poor (Urban Think Tank 2013). Once joined to existing infrastructure, it marks a rightful claim on space. This is its tectonics. So when residents begin to join materials to the existing concrete skeleton of the massive tower, the details of these joints read as a colonization of space by its new inhabitants. By accreting their own materials onto the structural framework of the tower, the residents signify their intention to remain. The two materials together read singularly and, at least conceptually, the building becomes theirs. It is a claim they have already proven willing to fight for and defend (see Anderson 2013; Urban Think Tank 2013).

This is not the case in Monrovia. There is in Monrovia an architectural vocabulary of appropriated space. But unlike Torre David, it is more unstable, less permanent. There is no material vocabulary for marking the permanent appropriation of infrastructure, no tectonic vocabulary that would allow for colonized spaces to be read as fully integrated and fully appropriated. In a brief but telling anecdote about the instability of architecture in Monrovia, Merran Fraenkel provides a useful example. One of the best-known and most financially successful shops in waterside in the 1960s was a zinc shack that had existed on the same spot for almost a hundred years. Despite its long tenure on the site, residents read the building not as a successful colonization of space but as an architecture of impermanence, since the legal ambiguities of land ownership meant that it could be swept away at any moment (see Fraenkel 1964: 49).

In the Ministry of Defense, in short, the relationship between the two elements of its construction would always be off kilter. The structure of the ministry continued to carry all the meaning of the permanence of the state, and the residents' infill remained saddled with a sense of impermanence and transitoriness. Despite the fact that many of them had resided in the building for a decade, this remained true until the day the ex-combatants living in the building were told to leave. And they did.

Impossible New Bodies

In the spring of 2012 it was still not certain what would happen to the Ministry of Defense building. A government draftsman had been dispatched to measure the structure and re-create the original blueprints that had been lost during the war. There were rumors of all stripes about the fate of the building, but none were any more convincing than the speculations of Major Sandi, the building's caretaker, who told me that he thought the monstrous structure might someday make a nice hotel.[3]

In his most famous essay on postmodernity, Fredric Jameson (1991) argued that John Portman's Westin Bonaventure Hotel in Los Angeles was the perfect embodiment of postmodern architecture. It was a building to be passed through, a building impossible to know how to inhabit. To dwell in the Bonaventure would require radical imagination and a whole new social landscape. It would require new bodies and new senses, and even that might not be enough. In the meantime, the building would simply be a space through which to move and to shop. Until Angelenos learned to "grow new organs . . . expand our sensorium and our body to some new yet unimaginable perhaps utterly impossible dimensions" (39), the Bonaventure would be a relay station in the networks of moving bodies and commodities through the city.

The Ministry of Defense is Monrovia's Westin Bonaventure. Not because it shares the Bonaventure's postmodern aesthetic, but because like the Bonaventure its architecture is impossible to comprehend. The ministry housed a population of ex-combatants and their dependents for more than a decade, but it was a population in transit, never a political community that could or would stake a more permanent, meaningful claim to the space around it. No one in the Ministry of Defense was actively seeking to "grow new organs."

There are, however, two important parentheticals to add to the story of the ministry's excessive architecture.

The first is that the ministry's inaccessibility has nothing to do with being ill suited to an African city. Modern architecture belongs in and to African cities no less than to cities anywhere on the planet. Whether or not there are more meaningful or appropriate vernacular architectures better suited to life on the continent is a separate debate.[4] But there is nothing distinctly African about being unable to lay claim to a space like the Ministry of Defense. If there are spaces in Monrovia in which it is impossible to know how to live, it is not because those forced to move through them are ill suited to modernity. It is because the modernity those forms represent is by definition uninhabitable.

A second note of caution lies in Major Sandi's odd proposition that the Ministry of Defense might someday make a fine hotel. There is, of course, sad poetry in a man squatting in a vast ruin imagining the building might someday house more affluent transients. But there is also a hint of possibility. The ex-combatants who resided in the Ministry of Defense could not imagine it as a space that belonged properly to them, a space that they could ever lay claim to and make their own. Certainly it was not a space they could imagine outside the terms established by Monrovia's modern political economy, in which the movement of young men and the labors of their bodies have become their sole productive resources.

But in her book on supermax prisons, the ultimate excessive architecture, Rhodes (2004: 90) describes how even there, making space uninhabitable is a continuous project of invention. The control prison may never become subject-producing space, but those contained within it cannot help but to continue to invent. They find ways to communicate with one another, dream new ways to attack their jailers, discover new weapons in the alien architecture that surrounds them. In response, an entire industry generates new prison architectures that mitigate the potential of inmates to experiment. Nothing on this landscape is fixed.

What this suggests is that there remains, even in the most extraordinary conditions, the potential to imagine a different set of possibilities for what a space can become. Imagining that the Ministry of Defense might one day house a luxury hotel is not a political claim on the building, not an act of resistance on behalf of a population violently excluded from the modern city. If anything, it replicates the logic that produced such marginality, a logic of inventing new ways to produce precarity among Monrovia's ex-combatant youth—hardly the material from which to build popular resistance, let alone a political movement. But it contains, at least, the hint that even here there may yet be an unimaginable urban future.

PHOTOGRAPHIC POSTSCRIPT

The Ministry of Defense is a building that belonged in totality to the military government of a young soldier. Its sweep and scale are superhuman, an expression of a certain mode of power derived from a combination of violence, privilege, and the occult. The result is a building that could not be meaningfully claimed even by those who had lived there for years after the war. The space itself exerted a kind of resistive agency that made it impossible to be anything other than what it was intended to be: an image of the all-powerful state.

In *Ministry of Defense #1* and *#4*, that extrahuman scale is evident in the grotesqueries of the seating area and the front entrance. There are enough reference elements in the images to underscore the absurd proportions and forms of these architectural features. The geometry of the stairwell in *Ministry of Defense #5* is similarly distended; in this case partly the product of the camera's wider than human focal length and partly the consequence of a severe and inhumanly proportioned design. The figures who appear in the various images, all ex-fighters who knew the space well, seem to become caricatures. None of them were deliberately

Ministry of Defense #1

Ministry of Defense #4

Ministry of Defense #5

Ministry of Defense #7

Ministry of Defense #8

arranged in the peculiar geometries they occupy in these pictures, but the way they were found and rendered by the camera visually overdetermines a layer of alienness and alienation from the space itself. Even the paper scraps in *Ministry of Defense #7* render the space hostile. The remnants of an earlier effort to domesticate the basement as living quarters by plastering its walls with newspaper and magazine images (a not uncommon practice of interior design around the continent), they seem especially bizarre and inadequate to the task in the Ministry of Defense. The advertisement from a New Jersey newspaper for an "executive business forum" might seem to belong to another world. But if it is a world that excluded the squatters who occupied the basement during and after the war, it was a world accessible to the upper echelons of Liberian society who constituted the Liberian state and to whom the building truly belonged.

It is in the images of the Ministry of Defense that the camera's role in architectural modernity is also the most obvious. In *Ministry of Defense #8*, the floor and ceiling are almost perfectly symmetrical mirrors reflecting one another over a void in the middle ground. The scale of the building is of course enormous, but the wide angle of the lens throws the repetition of the columns and the depth of the floor out of proportion. An already immense space feels even more so, as the wall and floor are made to converge and their dominance is exacerbated. The photograph, in other words, takes certain aspects of the design and overemphasizes them, though it does so subtly, so that this appears to be the logic of the space itself rather than a consequence of photography.

For anyone attempting to copy this design in a subsequent building, the elements that would most clearly make the space distinctive are the consequence of the optical effects of photography. If in some dystopian future the Ministry of Defense were to become canonical, generating imitations and interpretations and eventually its own architectural style, its copies would be in dialogue not with the ministry building but with the peculiar way that the camera renders symmetry and emptiness, the way it creates inhumanly proportioned space.

CHAPTER 3

E. J. Roye
The Corporate (Post)Modern

Field sketch #2, E. J. Roye Building

n a short 1970s propaganda film, *The Wealth of Liberia*, there is a brief glimpse of the E. J. Roye Building. It flashes past in a sequence of building exteriors in Monrovia. The baritone male voice of the narrator introduces the sequence by praising the Liberian government's commitment to "the principles and practice of free enterprise." He then goes on to describe the capital city's built environment as "a graceful cultural heritage. But a city as modern as today, the country having developed a fine balance between traditional African values and the modern way of life. Buildings steeped in the tradition of Liberia's rich history. Buildings reflecting the country's promise of a rich future. . . . Buildings that reflect the civic dignity of the city, its commerce and industry."[1] For the most part, the buildings that illustrate this fine balance are modernist blocks. One has a Romanesque row of columns across the front façade; another sports a generically African-motif fountain in its forecourt. But the architectural evidence of Liberia's commitment to "the principles and practice of free enterprise," to "civic dignity," and to "commerce and industry" is unmistakable. The aesthetic of the E. J. Roye and most of the other buildings that stand for the wealth of Liberia are American corporate modernism.

Two decades later, the E. J. Roye Building figures more prominently in a second film. *Liberia: An Uncivil War* (Brabazon and Stack 2008) documents the LURD advance on the capital city

E. J. Roye #1

E. J. Roye #2

FACING PAGE: *E. J. Roye #3*

E. J. Roye #4

E. J. Roye #5

and the intense fighting that preceded the intervention of Nigerian peace-keepers. The badly damaged building stands in the background as civilians and Charles Taylor's armed forces prepare for the rebels. When fighting reaches the bridge into downtown, Taylor's troops position themselves in the building and the camera periodically shifts to reflect their firing position and their vantage point on the city below.

The building and its connotations in the two films could not be more different. In the former, the E. J. Roye stands as testament to Liberia's prosperity and modernity. In the latter, it signifies a calamitous, violent postmodernity, the antithesis of a properly functioning economy or a modern urban existence. But the E. J. Roye Building itself links the two stories. Its American corporate modern aesthetic makes visible, and to some extent animates, an economic imaginary that makes these two different narratives of the city essentially the same. For at least some Monrovians in the postwar present, the skeletal form of the E. J. Roye is visual evidence that the story of modern Monrovia is the story of a violent economy—past, present, and future.

Forms of the Modern

The E. J. Roye Building stands on a ridge on the northeast side of downtown Monrovia. It looks out over Providence Island, the first site of settlement when the American Colonization Society repatriated former slaves to what is now Liberia in 1822. It is the most prominent landmark on the northern approach to the central business district. From a distance, the dominant feature of the structure is a central five-floor rectangular tower, one of the few structures of any height in the city. Topped by smaller boxes housing services and seated atop a multistory tiered plinth, the E. J. Roye is elegant and spare in its design, commanding in its site. It is in many ways a perfectly fitting expression of its program: a headquarters for the True Whig Party (TWP), the political vehicle for the oligarchs who ruled Africa's oldest democracy as a one-party state. Completed in 1965, the building's provenance resonates uncannily with themes that run through Liberia's history. It is named for the country's fifth president, Edward J. Roye, born in the United States of Igbo ancestry and an immigrant to Liberia. Roye's legacies include a disastrous loan organized without legislative approval, a failed attempt to extend his rule beyond constitutional limits, and an eventual coup d'état. By some accounts the E. J. Roye stands today on the site where Roye was executed one hundred years before the building was completed.[2] Ownership of the building has most recently been the subject of a dispute between the Ellen Johnson Sirleaf government, which has argued alternatively that the building was (secretly) publicly financed and therefore has always belonged to the Liberian state; that it was nationalized during the 1980 coup; and that it was purchased from the TWP sometime in the early 2000s. The TWP, by contrast, claims that the multiple sales and leases on the building have all been fraudulent and that the building remains private property (see, e.g., "Liberia: TWP Partisans" 2013).

Like many important modernist buildings, the E. J. Roye is the subject of a romantic, likely apocryphal story of its design origins and the visionary genius of its author. Winston Richards, a young Liberian architect working in the United States, was called back to the country by President William Tubman with the commission for the TWP headquarters, Richards's first major project in the country. His original design, according to legend, was sketched out on an unused dinner napkin during his transatlantic flight.[3]

Becoming the nation's senior architect and then deputy minister of public works, Richards went on to design some of the nation's most important public buildings. Many of these, like the international terminal at Roberts airfield and the central John F. Kennedy Medical Center, represent sophisticated expressions of the complexities of West African nationalism and statehood in the 1960s and early 1970s. In the E. J. Roye, the complex sociopolitical landscape of Cold War Liberian nationalism is captured in the programmatic and design tension between the horizontal and vertical spaces of the tower. The former, the massive plinth supporting the tower, mediates the complicated balance of public and private that characterized the one-party state at the height of the Cold War and the nation-building spirit of the 1960s. The latter, the rectangular tower, concretizes the ultimately failed promise of a purely rational free-market economy. It is worth considering each of these planes in turn.

THE HORIZONTAL

The plinth on which the E. J. Roye building sits abuts Ashmun Street, a central corridor in Monrovia's congested and cosmopolitan downtown grid. On its façade are a series of large bas-relief sculptures by Liberian artist, academic, and politician R. Vahnjah Richards. Multiple stories high, they offer heroic depictions of agricultural production and manual labor, captioned by nationalist platitudes.

E. J. Roye #6

E. J. Roye #7

E. J. Roye #8

E. J. Roye #9

FACING PAGE: *E. J. Roye #10*

E. J. Roye Building from Ashmun Street. 2005. The vision the building presents to the street, through both its art and its austere façade, is an image of an impregnable one-party state.

The plinth, given its scale, serves as the point of visual and physical contact between the building and the city from any point close to the structure. Owing largely to the success of Mies van der Rohe's Seagram Building in New York (1954–1958) and to regulations that cap the ratio of vertical to horizontal feet, such plinths have entered the standard vocabulary of modern American skyscrapers. In most tall buildings, a plinth is intended to both frame the tower and create the impression of a public space around it; in Mies's Seagram Building, the plinth is topped by fountains, benches, and greenery, all easily accessible from the street. As Aureli puts it, in rare cases like the Seagram Building the plinth provides a space in which to confront the city and explore the relationship between the individual structure and the urban flows that surround it, thus making it "one of the most intense manifestations of the political in the city" (2011: 37). In practice, plinths more often serve to isolate office or apartment towers from the surrounding street life, as well as contain parking and other private spaces and services. Those open spaces they create around the tower are tightly regulated and rarely, if ever, truly public.

Certainly this is the case with the plinth at E. J. Roye. Though it offers a commanding view over the northern reaches of the city, the open spaces atop the plinth are barren and mostly inaccessible. What the plinth presents to the city from the street below is fortresslike and monumental. It expresses the strength and impregnability of the political party and, by extension, the state, and it does so as an insurmountable vertical wall. There is no pretense of public or agonistic space, nothing that suggests encounter, dialogue, or difference. The plinth is adorned with public art, but its scale and didacticism only serve to make the building read more directly as an expression of government-mandated Liberian nationalism.

Inside, the distinction between the TWP and the Liberian state is further blurred. The plinth houses a massive auditorium. Set under huge concrete ceiling supports and lit by massive stained glass windows, the auditorium was presumably designed to give grandiosity and ceremony to party congresses, events that under presidents Tubman and Tolbert would have amounted to private negotiations over access to public wealth and power. But what most Monrovians I spoke with remembered of the space, indeed of the entire E. J. Roye Building, was a different kind of modern state making and nationalism: for years the auditorium was the setting of the hugely popular Miss Liberia pageant.

THE VERTICAL

In its form, place, and function, the plinth of the E. J. Roye offered a vision of the state as inseparable from the party, and presented both through an "aesthetics of vulgarity": oversized, spectacular, cartoonish, and powerful (Mbembe 1992). E. J. Roye's tower, on the other hand, visualizes state governance as a rational project of modern corporate management. The tower consists of a hidden service core of elevators, stairwell, pipes, and wiring, surrounded by a grid of virtually identical office cubes. Visible from nearly everywhere in the city at the time it was built, the repeating pattern of window openings transforms the logical Cartesian grid of the tower into a message of bureaucratic efficiency, a message as obvious from the outside as it is inside. Although elegantly massed, the tower signifies the rational, undramatic promise of functionalism and objectivity. Once again, the vocabulary is that of the American corporate skyscraper, an architecture called silent for the way it engages and facilitates the machinic dynamics of a modern economy without explicitly engaging its social or political context (see Aureli 2011: 34–38; Tafuri 1976: 148; Wallerstein 2008). Two narrow protrusions give some variation to the east and west façades of the E. J. Roye, but as a whole the tower expresses much the same thing as the repetitive patterns of the Seagram tower or any number of glass and steel corporate headquarters around the world. These are abstract but unchallenging forms that respond to the city around them not as a unique historical space with particular cultural or political dynamics. They respond instead to urbanization's need to rapidly and efficiently facilitate the exchanges of modern capitalism: "Their apparent indifference to context is paradoxically their true contextual quality, which reflects, in the most literal and objective terms, precisely what one cannot see: the generic space of exchange and reproduction behind the appearance of figural diversity" (Aureli 2011: 36).

It is not hard to imagine how captivating and appropriate this narrative was in early 1960s Monrovia. The city was arguably the most cosmopolitan and developed in West Africa at the time. As independence movements were sweeping the continent, Liberia stood out as a mature state with an already deep history of self-determination and modern governance. Iron ore mining, rubber production, and industrial agriculture were expanding and generating huge profits through greater mechanization and transportation efficiency (albeit profits directed primarily toward American companies). And, perhaps most importantly, Liberia was the United States' one unambiguous ally in the Cold War politics of West Africa, a proud and dogmatic advocate of U.S.-style "principles and practices of free enterprise."

TAKEN TOGETHER, WHAT THE PLINTH and tower in the E. J. Roye Building signify was a complex and thinly veiled fiction: that the Liberian economy was a freely functioning, rational machine driving the growth and development of a democratic state. In reality, sovereignty in Africa's oldest republic was exercised by a relatively small cadre of elites who blended public and private, state and personal in the classic model of big-man neopatrimonial governance funded by superpower patronage and the trade in Liberian natural resources (for more on this history, see Clapham 1976; Liebenow 1987; Reno 1998; Sawyer 2005). It is this reality that gave the E. J. Roye shape and meaning first as a 1960s modernist built form, and then as a 1990s postmodern ruin.

The Form of the Postmodern

Standing on the top floor of the E. J. Roye Building, looking north across the Johnson Bridge into the city's sprawling but relatively flat Bushrod Island neighborhoods, it was obvious that the very same elements that made the building an efficient conduit for relations of production and a powerful symbol of modern commerce—its height, site, and materials—also made it an excellent location from which to halt the 2003 LURD rebel advance on downtown.[4]

That advance was in many ways the logical outcome of the forms of economy celebrated and enabled by the E. J. Roye in the first place. The young men who fired on the building from across the bridge, and those who fired back from the empty window frames of its tower, were an "industrial reserve army" (Marx's term for the mobile and crisis-prone labor pool) that sustained West Africa's resource extraction economy and its warlord brand of politics (Hoffman 2011a, 2011b; Reno 1998). These were young men brought into the wars' various fighting factions most often as piecemeal subcontractors, seasonal and migrant workers who joined armed units between periods of work on the region's mines or other manual labor industries—and often via the same mechanisms of recruitment and mobilization (see Hoffman 2011b; Munive 2011). The urban siege of Monrovia was therefore not the failure of the vision behind E. J. Roye but its consequence.

A decade later, the building still seemed to embody that high modernist vision for the Monrovians with whom I spoke about it. Dee was old enough to remember attending the Miss Liberia pageant in the great hall of the E. J. Roye plinth. Driving toward the building along the same route LURD used in its march toward downtown, I asked her what she thought should be done with the E. J. Roye. She seemed incapable of speaking of the building in anything but the past tense. Dee described the E. J. Roye as the most sophisticated space in the city, part of the metropolitan gleam that distinguished the Monrovia of her childhood from the Monrovia she knew as a teenager and adult, a period in which she lived with a series of commanders in Taylor's militias before joining LURD. "I have lived in Accra and Lomé," she said, "but the E. J. Roye before the war was the most beautiful building in West Africa. As she went on to describe the nationalist pomp of the Miss Liberia pageant, it seemed clear that the object of nostalgia for her was, as Charles Piot (2010) has written about post–Cold War West Africa generally, the future itself. The E. J. Roye embodied a moment in which it was possible to imagine a West African future that could be understood through grand, modern auditoriums and national beauty pageants hosted by the patriarchs of a big man–led state. When I pressed Dee further on what should be done with the E. J. Roye now, she shrugged. "Buildings build up a nation also," she answered vaguely, and left it at that.

Francis, one of the few people still living in the building in 2012, was no more able to articulate a future for or through the structure. "You don't expect a building like this to be the heart of the city," he said, seated on the hard concrete bleachers near the ceiling at the back of the auditorium. "Just standing here for years and years in this condition." In the twelve years he claimed to have lived in the space, there had been a number of efforts to develop the property. The last one, four years before, had resulted in a mass eviction of squatters from the tower. But that scheme, like earlier ones, had collapsed when the developer ran out of money. Francis told the story as one of an eternal return, as though there were no other possible outcomes than that of fantastic real estate speculation followed by inevitable bust.

If the E. J. Roye failed to offer itself to Monrovians like Dee and Francis as a catalyst for articulating urban futures, it could nevertheless easily become the raw material for creative invention within the limited confines of how ex-combatant Monrovians imagined the present. Repeatedly as I moved around and within the space, I was witness to, and occasionally party to, small improvisations. Endlessly creative and inventive as these were, their creativity seemed only to reinforce the city's larger logical grid of monetized transactions and cautious, contingent relations.

The first time I entered the E. J. Roye to photograph the plinth and tower, an older man named Ibrahim was sitting outside. The three young men accompanying me were friends from the progovernment militias in Sierra Leone, young men who had subsequently joined LURD and were now living in Monrovia. We greeted the older man respectfully, but it was clear that he had no authority to either permit or prohibit us from entering. Nevertheless, Ibrahim asked us our names and our business. He wrote nothing down, but seemed to take careful mental note of everything we said. Ibrahim slipped inside a gate and disappeared around the back of the E. J. Roye, evidently off in search of someone who could pass judgment on our request to come in.

The old man's situation seemed obvious, and indeed he confirmed it when we met again later. Ibrahim had no official position anywhere, no relationship to the E. J. Roye or the TWP. But he was an elderly man with no money and little to do. He happened to be sitting nearby as we approached. There was no one around to stop or contradict him, and therefore no good reason he shouldn't, for that one moment at least, be the security guard at the E. J. Roye. Who owned the E. J. Roye, whether the building was public or private, what relevance it might have in the story I might tell of Monrovia were all secondary to the fact that for the moment Ibrahim stood profitably between us and the gate. He had played the role well enough, and the gamble paid off. My companions and I slipped him a small token when we left.

As we waited for Ibrahim to return, however, a more high-stakes and volatile negotiation unfolded in the building's shadow. Across the street from the E. J. Roye stands the skeleton of a second building, roughly equal in size. The National Bank was another monolith halted by the war. But in the bank's case, an American contractor had been found to oversee the refurbishment of the structure and the completion of the project. The site was fenced with a high corrugated zinc barrier and a private security company had stationed uniformed guards at the gate.

One of those guards approached us and demanded that we explain ourselves. The terrain of the conversation shifted quickly. The guard's questions were never directly answered. It seemed, in fact, that he never intended them to be. Instead my three companions and the guard began a long and heated argument about who had the right to ask questions, who had the right to move freely through the city streets, who had the right to photograph the city's buildings or even to look at them at will. All four men referenced their years spent "fighting for the country," though all of them were careful not to identify the factions to which they belonged. Two of my companions, Hassan and A. B., each produced identity cards that, they claimed, showed them to be members of the Liberian security services—Hassan in intelligence, A. B. in the antinarcotics unit, though neither title appeared anywhere on the cheaply laminated IDs. Mohammed, the third LURD ex-fighter, produced no card but hinted darkly that he belonged "to government." It was a free country, they claimed, and therefore they could stand in the road and look at the city if they so chose. They were, after all, members of the security service. Citizenship itself, as far as I could tell, meant nothing in respect to who could do what in the center of a municipal street or how one could relate to the city's built environment. But citizenship gave young men the right to belong to the state's security apparatus and that, in turn, connoted certain liberties.

The security guard pulled out his radio handset and baton, markers of his own legitimacy and authority. His orders were clear, he said, though he never specified what those orders were or why they pertained to us. But he had asked what we were doing and had been met with a challenge. He clearly intended to use whatever tools were at hand, symbolic or material, to take up that challenge. The shouting escalated to shoving, and then Ibrahim returned and motioned us inside the gate. Leaving the security guard talking into his radio, we quickly slipped in after him, bit players in a set piece of masculinity and improvisational urban belonging.

Arthur, Architect

Arthur was one of the few people I could find willing to directly address what might happen to the E. J. Roye in the future, and indeed one of the few who might imagine having any say in the matter. Arthur ran a small firm that was periodically contracted by the Ministry of Public Works to review drawings for public infrastructure projects. He expected that the plans for the E. J. Roye, if it ever was to be rebuilt, might pass through his office.

Over coffee I asked him what a future iteration of the structure should be. His response was an articulate mélange that both challenged and affirmed the processes of modernization and urbanization that the E. J. Roye has represented since the mid-1960s.

> You have to do something different with it. Certain areas within it they are not guaranteed [i.e., not safe]. So you have to break it and rebuild it new. This building is the old model. So you have to do something modern to make it nice. So many years ago, way back, almost thirty years ago [sic], this is the old design. So you have to give it a new face. To make the city nice. Because this is the capital city. You have to do the design that will

beautify the city. It's the tallest building. So the back and front have to be a very nice design so that anyone entering the city will know it is a beautiful building.

It is hard to imagine a clearer articulation of what has become the hegemonic view of the role of architecture in the modern city. The idea of the iconic building that brands the city, preferably one designed by an internationally renowned architect, has come to be known as the Bilbao Effect, following the perceived economic impact of Frank Gehry's Guggenheim Museum on the struggling Spanish city. But it is an approach to urban architecture that was the subject of critique for decades before. Critics like Manfredo Tafuri (1976) and (somewhat ironically) Rem Koolhaas (1978) argued that modern architecture had essentially devolved into efforts to give a new face to structures that housed unchanging relationships of production. Even radical-seeming architecture generally fails to challenge the grid of the city as a whole. Indeed, the more radical the individual pieces of this urban puzzle, the easier it becomes to sustain the homogeneity of the whole (see Aureli 2011: 21–26).

When I asked him to imagine what a beautiful building worthy of central Monrovia might look like, Arthur was unequivocal. The most beautiful buildings in Monrovia were currently those being built in the Sinkor neighborhood east of downtown. Considered one of the city's wealthiest and safest districts, Sinkor has in recent years seen a massive building boom, much of it in the form of corporate offices for banks, insurance companies, and parastatals. The aesthetic is overwhelmingly that of postmodern "decorated sheds" (Venturi, Scott-Brown, and Izenour 1972): simple boxes with exaggerated decorative façades, often of highly polished reflective glass and faux marble.[5] They are buildings perfectly suited to the functions they house. Where the E. J. Roye expressed the rationalization and industrialization of the Liberian economy under the firm hand of the Liberian neopatrimonial state, the postmodern architecture of Sinkor expresses the profitability of global flows of information, speculative financial instruments, and opaque banking practices. The built forms are gaudy but visually impenetrable, illogical, and poorly constructed.

"The problem with the E. J. Roye," Arthur went on, "is that everything is straight. In Sinkor you have steps. You have diagonals. It's very geometric. Compared to the Sinkor buildings, this one [the E. J. Roye] is not beautiful."

An Ahistorical War

At one point in the scenes of fighting over the bridge depicted in *Liberia: An Uncivil War*, there is a long shot of the E. J. Roye as seen from the rebel side of the bridge. Puffs of smoke escape repetitively from somewhere in the middle floors of the building. It is unclear whether they are the dust of impact from rebel fire or the exhaust from heavy artillery directed at the far side of the bridge. The façade of the E. J. Roye is pockmarked and mottled by multiple rounds of urban warfare over the past decade, so the rhythm that Winston Richards established in his façade has long since been broken. But together with the small bursts of smoke, the building in these images has a more complex counterpoint rhythm that expresses its history and logic more completely. It is an image that enshrines the place of violence in the story of Monrovian modernity.

I asked Arthur whether he thought there was any way to include that history in the redesign of the E. J. Roye. He thought for a moment, then shook his head. "Liberia doesn't have a proper history," he said sadly.

For Arthur, and perhaps for most Monrovians, history has indeed disappeared. The history that made E. J. Roye's corporate modern aesthetic make sense at the time it was built, a history that included a prosperous future of logical modernization and development, has been rendered absurd to older residents of the city and has never existed for most of the young men who occupied the building during the war.

For the same reason, the war itself is largely ahistorical. It seemed to go nowhere, and for many young people the end of fighting has not produced a material change in their lives or their prospects in the city. Certainly it gave them no alternative vision to the one that saw the E. J. Roye as a ruin space out of which they might invent some meager, fleeting possibilities. It offered them no vision of a new relation to the city. "We have no history" seems, in the end, a fitting diagnosis of an urban form that symbolized both the fictions of a modernity built on the promise of "the principles and practice of free enterprise" and a postmodernity built on violence.

PHOTOGRAPHIC POSTSCRIPT

A grid with particularly strong vertical elements dominates the geometry in virtually every image of the E. J. Roye Building. In each image it is scaled differently. In *E. J. Roye #3*, it is most pronounced at the diminutive scale of the tiling on the hallway

E. J. Roye #5

E. J. Roye #6

E. J. Roye #7

E. J. Roye #3

wall, turned golden by the setting sun. In *E. J. Roye #6*, the grid is massive, the result of intersecting concrete structural members that create the vast space of the auditorium.

But in every image the grid also breaks apart, or stands in contrast to elements whose own geometry is more complex or formless. The repetitive office cubicles of *E. J. Roye #5* are interrupted by the shattered wall, remnants of which are heaped on the floor. The rhythm of space is broken as well by the more haphazard lines and shapes of the river and the city below. And there is the absurd antigeometry of the missing exterior wall, the line that should keep the square of the office closed but instead opens precariously onto a void.

As a series of ethnographic images, the E. J. Roye series works through this interplay of geometries imposed, accidental, and interrupted. The ethnographic story of the building is a story of bureaucratized design. It is the story of a high modernist fantasy of regularization and efficiency, a story of capitalism devoid of politics, culture, or place. It is a fantasy that sowed the seeds of its own destruction, not because it failed but because to some degree it succeeded.

What is left today is a structure in which the camera cannot help but produce images that include both geometries, the pure geometry of the corporate modern ideal and the more chaotic geometry of the subsequent crisis. In contrast to narratives of a region retreating from modernity, descending to a primitive tribal state (the narrative that has dominated both textual and visual reportage from contemporary Liberia), *E. J. Roye #7* argues that the nomos of West African postmodernity is sensible only within the organizing framework of West Africa's earlier modernity. As two figures navigate their way through the pooled water and detritus of the once grand entrance hall of Monrovia's most cosmopolitan space, preparing petty goods for sale in the streets of the city, they become representatives of two opposed but complementary organizations of a contemporary West African political economy.

CHAPTER 4

Hotel Africa
The Uncritical Ruin

Field sketch, Hotel Africa

The Hotel Africa is a building in negative. From a distance, it appears unkempt but solid. It is surrounded by wild foliage but still perches majestically between the city and the sea.

On inspection, however, the Hotel Africa is a ghost. As periodic waves of violence swept through the northern suburbs of Monrovia in the early 2000s, slum dwellers around the hotel picked the complex apart, harvesting the building's useful or salable materials. In a relatively short period of time the hotel disintegrated, eaten away from inside. The rebar is gone from the concrete floors and walls. Wiring channels are excavated throughout the building. Door frames stand empty, balcony rails removed, tile chipped away, and windowpanes extracted with varying degrees of care. The outlines of the grand hotel complex can be traced down to minute details, but they are an absent presence. What remains is dust holding shape.

Even more than the E. J. Roye, the Ministry of Defense or the LBS, the Hotel Africa is a ruin. It is a recognizable form and at the same time completely barren. It exists but is useless. The hotel was once an important part of Monrovia's city story, but it has no obvious function in the urban present. And yet it remains an object of fascination, appearing again and again in news stories of contemporary Liberia and in Monrovians' accounts of their prewar past. The Hotel Africa, like all ruins, would seem to be

Hotel Africa #1

Hotel Africa #2

Hotel Africa #3

pregnant with meaning, though exactly what meaning is unclear. "The ruin is a ruin," write Julie Hell and Andreas Schönle, "precisely because it seems to have lost its function or meaning in the present while retaining a suggestive, unstable semantic potential" (2010: 6).

Finding the "semantic potential" in ruins is rarely a simple exercise in analyzing physical forms. The significance in the ruin lies in the always unfinished, unfolding stories of which it is a part (see Beasley-Murray 2010; Cairns and Jacobs 2014; Gordillo 2011, 2014; Larkin 2008; Stoler 2008, 2013). Reading ruins is therefore a narrative process, an art of combining historical and material fragments, real and imagined, into meaningful stories about the past, the present, and the future.

And yet, as architect and historian Andrew Herscher puts it, violence directed at the built environment is itself a kind of architecture. Ruin forms, especially those deliberately ruined, are more than just the index of other, more significant structural forces. The damaged buildings and monuments of Kosovo, Herscher's case study, were not simply the canvas on which ethnic differences played out in the second Balkan war of the 1990s. Constructing ruins by attacking existing architecture was an active part of building identities within the conflict. Ruins, like all built forms, are social, political, and economic productions and socially, politically, and economically productive. It is therefore possible, "even necessary," Herscher writes, "to understand [destruction] via the particular interpretive protocols of architecture" (2010a: 2; see also Herscher 2010b). It is not enough to see the ruin simply as evidence of larger processes of ruination, to use Ann Stoler's (2008, 2013) terminology. There is meaning in the form of the ruin itself.

Reading what remains of the Hotel Africa as meaningful architecture, however, is not easy. The hotel has not been appropriated or reworked to fit local needs or tastes, as has the modernist architectural legacy in any number of other African cities (see Avermaete, Karakayali, and von Osten 2010; Denison, Guang, and Gebremedhin 2007; Enwezor 2010). Nor does it fall into the ambiguous category of vernacular architecture, a term intended to recognize the creativity and dignity in everything from rural huts to urban slums (Bourdier and Minh-ha 2011; de Maat 2009; Neuwirth 2004; see also Chan 2012). Unrecognized as architecture, it can be challenging to see Monrovia's modern ruins as more than a metaphor for Monrovia's decline, rather than as an agent in the city's social, political, and economic processes. The hotel appears instead as a pile of rubble, a by-product of a long war and the background to the daily struggles of urban life.

But if it is a mistake to dismiss Monrovia's ruins out of hand, it would be equally shortsighted to overstate their potential importance. The contemporary preoccupation with ruins, and particularly the fascination with the modern ruin as a site of subversive, critical possibilities, runs the risk of romanticizing forms like the Hotel Africa. Not all ruins are the same. The ideal of a space open to almost unlimited experimentation and inventive possibilities seems misplaced in the Hotel Africa. The building is not likely to have what Rebecca Solnit called a ruin's "generative death like the corpse that feeds flowers" (2005: 88–90; cited also in La Cecla 2012: 42).

The difficulty in imagining the Hotel Africa as a generative ruin has less to do with the extent to which it is damaged than with how its ruins exist on the urban landscape. Both the narrative surrounding the building and the ruin form it produced place certain limits on the imaginative labor that could be done with it after the war. It may be true that all ruins have an unstable semantic potential, but it is no less true that the ruin as object asks for certain readings and places certain limits on its own interpretative possibilities.

For understanding the political imagination in Monrovia today, it is the second of these misreadings—the idea that a ruin like the Hotel Africa could hold a certain critical, politically subversive potential—that is the more interesting and consequential to explore. The various attacks on the city during the 1990s and early 2000s included a good deal of targeting of the city's built environment, with the various fighting factions using damage to buildings and infrastructure as evidence of their power and commitment to their cause (see Hoffman 2004). Deciding the future of the postwar city is therefore in large measure a question of reckoning with the material legacy of ruination as a mode of modern warfare. Urban design in a city like Monrovia has to be a project of reclamation and creative reuse, a project of envisioning "the city yet to come" (Simone 2004) from fragments and debris. Monrovia would seem an ideal urban landscape in which to explore and to invent new ways of inhabiting urban forms. But the Hotel Africa largely refuses to offer itself as grist for the critical project of imagining and inventing the "aftermodern" African city (Enwezor 2010).

Hotel Africa #5

Hotel Africa #6

FACING PAGE: *Hotel Africa #4*

The Silent Ruin

It was impossible to find anyone in the informal settlement surrounding the Hotel Africa willing to talk about the building's reverse construction. In Monrovia, a city of half-built and half-demolished forms, a city in which nothing falls entirely out of circulation, this silence is unusual. Among Monrovians there is a remarkable degree of openness about wartime appropriations of all manner of material, building materials included.[1] The line between survival and opportunism during and after the war could be very hard to locate, and while few people will admit to outright wartime looting, many have stories of scavenging, bricolage, improvisation, and appropriation. Yet with the Hotel Africa, these stories were virtually impossible to find.

There may have been a certain pragmatic caution at work here. For more than three decades the hotel was associated with wealthy expatriates and Monrovia's business and political elites. While it seemed unlikely that there could be any repercussions for those who had picked the building apart, one could not be certain. The "social life of things" (Appadurai 1988) in Monrovia can be unpredictable. Asking around the small community, everyone I spoke with claimed to have moved there only after the building was dismantled, or to have fled during the last rebel advances. There were many stories about the hotel's illustrious early days and its more infamous recent past. But about the building's deconstruction, no one would say a word.

This absence is a striking contrast to the building's prominent place in the story of Monrovia over the past few decades. The Hotel Africa's massive central block and its spread of detached villas, conference halls, casino, and Africa-shaped swimming pool once made it one of the most celebrated structures in the region. It was, for a time, the largest hotel in Liberia and one of two five-star resorts in the capital. Although less famous internationally than its counterpart the Ducor Intercontinental Hotel, it nonetheless achieved a degree of infamy, first as the grandiose backdrop to the 1979 Organization of African Unity conference and then as a hedonistic refuge for foreigners and Liberia's underworld during the war. Under the Charles Taylor presidency, the hotel was owned by Guus van Kouwenhoven, a Dutch businessman charged in 2006 with trading arms for Liberian timber in defiance of a UN ban. Adolphus Dolo, or General Peanut Butter (see chapter 1), served as the building's head of security. The hotel features in a number of NGO and UN reports as a meeting site for international traffickers. During the first phase of the Liberian war in the early 1990s, the journalist Mark Huband described the hotel as the last outpost for foreigners who would not or could not leave Liberia despite the growing risks: "The hotel attracted Liberia's seedy underbelly; anybody who ventured to the hotel was guaranteed a good time at discount rates" (1998: 180).

Whether the Hotel Africa's neighbors feared the possible return of Taylor and his associates, or whether they simply preferred not to risk upsetting the stability of the present by speaking too much of a painful past (see Shaw 2007a, 2007b), there were few stories to be found about the hotel's rapid transformation from redoubt to ruin.

Unlike the Ducor Hotel in the center of town, the Hotel Africa never properly belonged to the city. Harder to access and invisible from most of town, the Hotel Africa was well known but not a part of the visual landscape that most Monrovians encountered every day. Whereas the Ducor and other luxury architecture in the city became part of the aspirational narrative of Monrovia as a modern city, the Hotel Africa belonged more completely to a small clique of cosmopolitan Liberians and expatriates. Its form was less imbued with the narratives of national development, pride, and imagination. This was evident even in the building's death. When I asked one area resident about the Hotel Africa's wartime fate, he pointed to the widespread corruption of interim president Gyude Bryant's postwar government. "The community people said 'we will not also lose.' They saw the big people taking out [i.e., looting the country], they also took things out. . . . Can you imagine? Hotel Africa. A place that was well known all over West Africa, and you tear it down! That is not patriotism. We just don't care."

For an observer trying to divine meaning in the ruins of the hotel, even unstable meaning, what was left was the form of the structure itself. Like many modern ruins, especially those on the scale of a grand hotel complex, that form was fantastically surreal. From the central stairwell, the Hotel Africa's floors appear as vast expanses of mounded rubble, the interior and exterior walls mostly removed. Only the support columns remain. It is a strangely inviting landscape. The hard materials of construction have been pulverized and sit like mounds of sand in the air. The reinforcing steel rods have been ripped from the concrete, leaving a patchwork of holes and unsupported slabs under the debris. Since the hotel was vacated, an unknown number of gleaners have died after falling through hidden holes in the floors.

Hotel Africa #8

FACING PAGE: *Hotel Africa #7*

There is remarkable precision in the way the electric and plumbing channels have been uncovered in the remaining vertical surfaces of the hotel. Standing in the massive central lobby, it is easy to map the contours of the normally hidden service elements of the building, as though technical drawings have been used as the building's interior finish. By contrast, it is almost impossible to say how large the grand stairway leading to the lobby's balcony might have been. Today it is simply a thin ribbon of contorted concrete. The hotel's most distinctive and storied feature, its swimming pool shaped in the silhouette of the African continent, seems especially grotesque and kitschy when filled with only a shallow depth of black rainwater.

As in all ruins, the effect is unsettling, but for reasons not immediately clear. Because the hotel has not crumbled with age and has not been blasted with heavy artillery, it does not demand the obvious responses of other ruins: melancholia, nostalgia, outrage. It is a discomforting but provocative building, in its death as it was during its decades of life.

Reading Ruins

Given its history, the Hotel Africa might seem an unlikely catalyst for deep critical reflection. But in philosophy and anthropology, in politics, in art and architecture, ruins are often just that. In secular European thought this has been true, in one form or another, at least as far back as the Renaissance. In the early twentieth century, the ruins of Greek and Roman buildings were an important inspiration for Le Corbusier and other figures in modern movement architecture as they developed their ideals of pure geometry and honest form. In the early twenty-first century, ruins seem no less revolutionary and potent as a tool for analysis and critical thinking: in the aftermath of September 11, 2001; in the wake of urban economic catastrophes and "urbicide" (see Coward 2009) in eastern Europe and the Middle East; in the shadow of U.S. imperial practices and the rise of "disaster capitalism" (Klein 2007), ruins often serve as evidence of gross inequality and injustice.

For many contemporary observers, writing in the tradition of critical theorists such as Walter Benjamin and Georg Simmel, the potential in today's ruins therefore lies in their capacity to critique modernity and, more specifically, modern capitalism. Abandoned, abject, or appropriated built forms make visible the false promises on which capitalist economies and capitalist imaginations are built: that revolutionary technologies will remain so forever; that commodities exist independently of the relations of production that make them; that a place among nations can be secured through free-market principles and rational design. The ruins of modern forms challenge these narratives. They force modern urbanites to confront the "normative meanings" (Edensor 2005b: 323) in the forms and objects that make up the modern city. Ruins lead those who encounter them to question the promises and premises that are the fantasy life of the modern urban economy.

And equally important, a city's modern ruins challenge those who confront them to imagine what might come next. If ruins work as a space of critique, or at very least as a catalyst for critical thinking, this has as much to do with their relationship to the future as to the past. As Tim Edensor puts it in his work on Britain's industrial infrastructure, now a touchstone in the study of modern ruins, the industrial ruin requires a different orientation, physically and conceptually, to urban space. "Stripped of their use and exchange values and the magic of the commodity, they [modern ruins] can be reinterpreted anew . . . and they provoke speculation about how space and materiality might be interpreted, experienced and imagined otherwise" (Edensor 2005b: 330).[2] Ruins may be matter from the past out of place in the present, but as objects useful to think with, their primary orientation is toward the future.

Though this process of imagining the future differently is clearly an immaterial form of labor, it is built on the very material acts of occupying and engaging with the physical spaces of ruins. Benjamin's assertion that the modern ruin could exist as a form of critique was the product of wandering the Paris arcades in the first decades of the twentieth century (see Buck-Morss 2013; Leslie 2006). His scattered notes and fragmentary writings on the ruins develop first of all from his observations of these structures as they existed. They were, in his words, "caves containing fossils of an ur-animal presumed extinct" (Benjamin 1982: 1048, cited in Buck-Morss 2013). To make the ruin function as critique, as an indictment of the processes that led to ruination, Benjamin focused on material traces of destruction, the footprints of the ruining forces that rendered a structure useless or obsolete. In the case of the arcades, this was the expansion of the spectacular magic of commodities on display. As advertising became more and more a part of the generic urban fabric of the city, the arcades fell into disrepair and, rendered redundant, were layered over with dust and age.

Hotel Africa #9

Hotel Africa #10

In the 1990s the wars in Bosnia and Kosovo produced even more dramatic examples of actively building ruins. Herscher's (2010b) ethnographic account of Kosovo and the architectural theorist Lebbeus Woods's (1993; see also Rao 2007) projects on Sarajevo focus on the damage violence does to the built environment. Each identifies wartime destruction as a form of architecture. This "war-chitecture" is a process of designing and constructing meaningful spaces by violently reorganizing or marking existing spaces. Because the work of small arms, heavy artillery, graffiti, fire, or defacement reworks the built environment and never simply destroys it, these processes too become legible in the way ruins take shape. Like Benjamin's arcades, one can read these landscapes and from them develop a critical lens on the processes of ruination that formed them.

The bullet-, smoke-, and graffiti-scarred buildings across Sierra Leone and Liberia's cities are an obvious parallel. Even though much of the region's built environment exists in a state of permanent incompletion, constantly morphing between being built and falling apart, it is relatively easy to map wartime damage. These elements author the ruin, giving it a certain legibility and putting it within a wartime narrative. The names of militia or military units scrawled on the walls of occupied spaces name the agents that constructed the ruins, but even more importantly they name the processes of ruination: these are buildings designed and constructed by wartime violence. Their meaning may remain unstable, in Hell and Schönle's terms, but it is anchored in a particular history, and thus a particular narrative regimen, of war. It is an authored ruin, bearing the inscriptions of military occupation and sudden attacks during a prolonged dirty war (Gberie 2005).

The industrial forms of modern Europe or North America bear the traces of a different kind of ruination and thus belong to a different aesthetic, though they, too, are ruins. The damage of abandonment and dereliction are a different kind of architecture from the war-chitecture of West Africa or the Balkans. The abandoned forms of office towers and factories are prominent features of the cityscapes of small and medium-sized towns across the Global North. They are ruins. But in the material traces that remain, one can read the larger structural violence of downsizing, layoffs, closures, and decline. The walls of abandoned office towers bear the marks of the carefully removed paraphernalia of white-collar labor. In factory ruins there is a visible narrative of machinery disassembled, of useful bits and pieces carefully extracted

War graffiti, Tubmanburg, Liberia. 2005. Throughout the Mano River war, the various factions used graffiti as a form of signature, laying claim to the ruins they had created.

and stored for an uncertain future. These are the remnants of methodical processes of leaving and obsolescence. They, too, are authored ruins. Reading them is an archaeological process, a project of reconstructing the past from material clues. But these clues serve as evidence in support of familiar narratives: narratives of economic catastrophe unfolding more or less slowly over decades.

Like Benjamin's Parisian arcades, moldering in the early twentieth century after their nineteenth-century novelty had worn off, these are modern ruins that can function as critique because the authoring processes of their ruination are so visible within the material traces that remain. Although there are many different versions of the Sierra Leone and Liberia war story, the ruins that conflict generated bear the marks of a young man's war. The graffiti-scrawled walls and recklessness of the destruction in the Mano River warscape lend themselves to multiple critical readings: of a style of irregular warfare in which private, civilian spaces are the primary battleground; of a media-saturated environment in which young men perform violence by creating ever more outrageous spectacles; even of a failed education system.[3] But their interpretive possibilities are not limitless. They read unequivocally as war damage.

There is an equal number of versions of the story of Global North eco-

Abandoned office tower, Lugo, Italy. 2014. The signifying practices of economic ruination are clearly visible in cities of the Global North.

War graffiti, Kailahun, Sierra Leone. 2001. The wartime architecture of ruin in Sierra Leone and Liberia spoke eloquently of a young man's war, a war in which civilian spaces were the primary battlefields.

Abandoned vinegar factory, Lugo, Italy. 2014. The violence of industrial obsolescence remains legible in the factory ruin.

nomic decline, but modernist ruins serve in each of them as critical evidence of an unsustainable and unhealthy political economy. Abandoned factories and office towers directly refute the promises of labor security, efficiency through technological innovation, and economic expansion without sacrifice that are so important to the modern global economy.

In short, different material ruins make for different stories of ruination. The ruin itself exercises agency in the interpretive uses to which it can be put. Therein lies the problem of ruins like the Hotel Africa.

The Unauthored Ruin

In contrast to other ruin sites, the Hotel Africa says little about its own ruination. As ruins they are unauthored. With neither physical traces nor a circulating narrative in which to be anchored, the remaining form of the Hotel Africa is unusually silent. The thin line of the once grand central stair, the missing pieces of balconies, the webs of wires and pipes chiseled from the walls and structural steel mined from the floors make it possible to understand the form the building once took, but they are not architecture in the way of other ruins. They do not make meaning as the deliberate desecration of mosques and churches in Kosovo or Sarajevo made meaning during the

Balkan wars. They are not the war-chitecture created by the fighting factions in Sierra Leone and Liberia as they produced ruin forms by setting fire to the built environment of Freetown, Monrovia, Voinjama, or Bo. Nor are they the obsolescent European architecture of economic collapse. The ruination of the Hotel Africa cannot be divined from its ruins. They are simply a building in negative, a ruin without authorship.

As such, they would seem to be largely unavailable as a form of critique. They stand as testament for or against nothing. The ruination of the E. J. Roye building is clearly legible in the way its façade bears the scars of mortar fire and its interior is marked by the material detritus of military encounters. The LBS and the Ministry of Defense both retain the traces of their domestication by squatters. They reflect their histories as ruin and their processes of becoming ruin, the larger webs of physical and imaginative acts that produced their ruin form. In these structures is a kind of architectural evidence that may be ambiguous or ambivalent (their "unstable semantic potential") but that nevertheless dictates certain readings of the ruin and its ruination. The same cannot be said of the Hotel Africa.

In truth the Hotel Africa always existed on the far side of the gulf that separated most Monrovians from the international and domestic elite. It was legible to most Monrovians only as a surreal form that belonged to a different order. Now that its skeletal form has been picked clean, it continues to exist as an indecipherable form, the narratives of which are mostly unknowable.

Because it is a ruin that cannot be read as critique, because it offers no way to understand or interpret its process of ruination, the Hotel Africa also offers no vision of an alternative future. It is not a space in which, as Edensor says of derelict British factories, "the becomings of new forms, orderings, and aesthetics can emerge" (2005a: 15; see also Doron 2000, 2007). This is not simply because the building is unsafe to occupy, but because there is nothing against which those who might occupy it can be defined or can define themselves. The squatters, artists, anarchists, even the flora and fauna that might pass through and make use of other modern ruins create meaningful new forms in opposition to the failed, "normative" meanings inscribed all around them (see La Cecla 2012: 12–14). Where they work as critique, ruins are what Deleuze and Guattari (1987) called deterritorializing "war-machines," creative, active forces that undo the codes and dominant orders in which they have been inscribed. War-machines exist because they have an organization of power to work simultaneously with and against. The radical new possibilities they give rise to represent an escape from something. For the ruin to become active space in this Deleuzian sense, to become part of "the city yet to come" (to appropriate AbdouMaliq Simone's [2004] memorable characterization of the inventiveness of African urbanity), it must bear the material markings of its becoming-ruins and reflect a failed promise and history. Caracas's Torre David tower, the Freetown Christiania settlement in Copenhagen, Vatnsstigur 4 in Reykjavik, Corviale in Rome—each of these better-known critical ruins were possessed and transformed as a response to a city's pressing housing needs. But their experiments in citizenship and urban living were crafted in dialogue with the evident, material processes of exclusion and ruination that were written on the buildings themselves.

In a review of Guy Tillim's (2005) photographs of the ruin landscape of Johannesburg and other southern and central African cities (Tillim 2009), Okwui Enwezor (2007, 2010) argues that Tillim's images of squatters inhabiting once modern apartment blocks and office towers, remaking the appropriated spaces to suit their own needs, desires, and capabilities, are a kind of ethnography of an emergent African "aftermodernity." The new architecture of this decidedly African form of urban habitation is a creative project, a productive experiment in living. It is not simply the failure of European modernism as manifest in Africa, but is instead an unfinished project of crafting something new from the material ruination that is the colonial and postcolonial legacy in African cities. But aftermodernity is still a critical vision of the modernist ruin. The architecture it envisions is a direct response to the unfulfilled promises written and still legible in the skyscrapers, monuments, housing schemes, and public buildings of the high modernist moment in Africa. "It disowns and dispossesses the colonial inheritance" (Enwezor 2010: 616) by reworking the possibilities that once existed and still remain as latent traces in modernism's built forms.

By contrast, the only new architectures produced by the deconstruction of the Hotel Africa are spread thinly around the city. They are found in the bricolage structures assembled from the carted-away bits of what was once a significant Monrovia landmark. What is left is unreadable. It is form without critical possibility, more rubble than ruin.

Dreamworlds

This is not to say that the Hotel Africa cannot be employed symbolically for constructing arguments about the future. But with no critical potential, that future vision would seem destined to be a reactionary one. The anonymous reporter whose article "Dead with Kaddafi" appeared in the May 30, 2013, edition of the *New Republic*, a Monrovia newspaper, certainly regarded the Hotel Africa as a ruin. The bulk of the piece is based on the author's visit to the Ducor Hotel, though he or she references "the completely ruined" Hotel Africa as further evidence of Monrovia's "general state of devastation." Part travelogue, part history, part editorial, the piece begins with the death of Libyan leader Muammar Gaddafi in 2011. Describing Gaddafi's legendary "generosity" toward the rest of Africa over four decades, the author declares that "the Hotel has died with the former Libyan strongman." Gaddafi, according to rumors in Monrovia, had pledged to rebuild the Ducor, the Hotel Africa, and other major Monrovian infrastructure. Given the current state of all of these buildings, the author says, "this is a task so huge for the [Liberian] government to handle" that in all likelihood the efforts to rehabilitate any of these structures cannot now proceed. Monrovia's landmark built environment "is history and it could remain as such."

The article is a striking articulation of just what can and cannot be imagined with the unauthored ruins of the Hotel Africa. Gaddafi's proposed intervention in contemporary Liberia was a vestige of the "high modernist" (Scott 1998) forms of political engagement that had been so significant across the continent for decades. The Libyan leader's vision of Pan-Africanism had resulted not only in generous handouts for infrastructure developments across West Africa, but also in direct interventions through training and arming dissident groups, including those most involved in the Sierra Leonean and Liberian fronts of the Mano River war (see Abdullah 1998; Ellis 1999; Gberie 2005; Rashid 2004; Richards 1996). Gaddafi's was a dictatorial vision of political power and sweeping, utopian master planning. But it was of a piece with U.S. and Soviet interventions in Africa during the Cold War, and the European colonial projects before them. Like the rhetoric surrounding Charles Taylor and the possibilities of his return to set things straight in Liberia (see chapter 5), what each of these fantasy "dreamworlds" (Buck-Morss 2000) represented was a political imagination of large-scale, often violent reorganization, a sweeping away of the past and wholesale rebirth.

The fact that the author of "Dead with Kaddafi" suggests that the end of this kind of patronage support quite possibly meant the end of hope for Liberia is both unsurprising and deeply disturbing. What he or she voices is a conservative, reactionary fantasy that flourishes not only when the actual processes of ruination are ignored, but when those processes cannot be easily located in the material forms that ruination produces. The Hotel Africa would be a difficult, perhaps impossible site from which to articulate an alternative political vision along the lines imagined by Edensor, Enwezor, or Solnit. The hotel fails to offer itself as useable evidence of the internal crises or contradictions of the economy that created it as a luxury space in a poor West African nation. Nor does it serve as a legible indictment of the violence that re-created it as ruin. Unable to read the hotel's unauthored ruins as a form of critique, the author of "Dead with Kaddafi" is unable to use those ruins to articulate a novel political vision. Instead, what fills the silence around the Hotel Africa and other unauthored, unreadable ruins is a utopian fantasy that modernity's detritus can be ignored, and some unfettered master planner can build the world anew on its ashes.

PHOTOGRAPHIC POSTSCRIPT

Like the building itself, the images that make up the Hotel Africa series are the most haunted — both by the past and by the nature of photographic renderings of space.

One human figure appears throughout the series. He is a young man who lives not far from the hotel. He doesn't know much about the hotel's history, but makes a few Liberian dollars now and again by warning visitors (mostly expatriates) not to walk across the floors of the upper stories.

In *Hotel Africa #4*, *#7*, and *#10*, he performs certain of the functions common to human figures in architectural renderings and in architectural photography. He gives scale to the surroundings. He draws attention to how a body might move through or occupy a space. He animates an otherwise largely inanimate scene.

At the same time, he does none of the things that a human body has been called upon to do in other architectural photographs. The characters who populate the photographs of Julius Shulman and other well-known midcentury architectural modernists were aspirational. They linked the architecture not simply to modernity but to an elite kind of modernist consumption that was a fantasy even for those who could ostensibly afford it. The young man in the Hotel Africa images is not

Hotel Africa #4

Hotel Africa #6

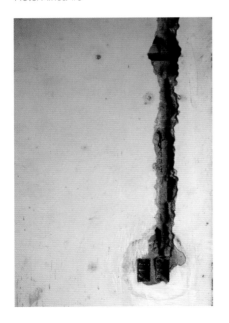

Hotel Africa #8

Hotel Africa #5

Hotel Africa #7

Hotel Africa #10

that. Nor is he is a disciplining figure from Eichler-era advertising photographs, instructing viewers in how to live in their new, unfamiliar but cutting-edge surroundings. And finally, he is not a figure from an Iwan Baan photograph. He performs no mundane, everyday tasks. He does not argue implicitly through his body and his activities that architecture is simply one element on a stage set of the city.

The young man is a ghost in these images. He most closely resembles the highly abstract forms that an architect might use in location sketches or early concept drawings. He is a shorthand figure to suggest that life takes place, or that it did so once. Properly scaled, he represents an argument that the space is oriented toward human habitation. It is properly proportioned to the human body; its places of flow and rest are logical and defined; it is a structure of human dwelling. But it is these things only in potential or in the past. Like the Hotel Africa itself, all we can say about the young man in these images is that he exists, or at least that he once did. Nothing more.

The ambiguity of destruction in the remainder of the series underscores the extent to which the building is a ruin that cannot be reclaimed. This is its anthropological argument: that not all ruins can be put toward new uses, made to be the grounds for a critique of the processes of ruination. In *Hotel Africa #5* or *#8* the reality of damage is obvious. But the mechanics of ruin are not. The ruin processes are not especially careful, but they are too precise to be a recognized form of violence. Whatever dug out the wiring channels of *Hotel Africa #8* did so without malice. But it also did so without the cynical, clinical precision of industrial downsizing and obsolescence. Evidence that would point toward the agent of this particular haunting is nowhere to be found in the images. Here, too, nothing meaningful remains.

The sole image that might offer a counterreading, *Hotel Africa #6*, a photograph of cards scattered on the rubble of the stairwell, takes a moment to understand. It would seem, at first glance, to be some kind of meaningful clue—a card game frozen at the moment of violence that generated this ruin space. Uncertain evidence, but evidence nonetheless that traces of a life interrupted—and how and by what—might be divined from what remains. But even that meager possibility leads nowhere. The photograph is an interpretation of an obvious trope in ruin photographs: everyday objects made alien and extraordinary by the death of the building that contains them. But on closer inspection, it is a misinterpretation. The cards are too clean. They have been dropped and settled at some point after the work of damage was done. They belong to a different geological stratum than the rubble beneath. They are not fossils made by some cataclysmic event, nor have they weathered and aged on the same arc as their surroundings. They came later, at some indecipherable moment and for some undecidable reason that would seem to have nothing to do with the ruin processes of the building itself. Whatever ethnographic evidence the cards provide is unreadable in the image, just as the ruin that contains them is unreadable in the landscape of the city.

CHAPTER 5

Liberia Broadcasting System
Three Utopias

LBS -backside

Field sketch, LBS

The Liberia Broadcasting System building sits fortress-like on a hilltop at the eastern edge of Monrovia. From the highway below, everything about the building speaks to state aggrandizement. Like the Ministry of Defense, it is a brutalist building, at least as seen from outside. Four identical corner towers and almost perfectly symmetrical façades make the LBS a hulking concrete square, its only variation a massive carport that extends from and shades the front entrance. As a whole it seems a near-perfect expression of government fantasies of unassailability. To reach the LBS today, the easiest route is on foot up the steep hillside, threading between hovels of zinc, mud, and burlap. The approach only makes the LBS building appear more mythical and surreal.

In early 2012 some eighty-five families still lived in the LBS. None of them intended to stay much longer, though most had been in the building for years. Martin, the vice chairman of the LBS Residents' Association, told me that the vertical settlement's population was ready to move on. They had neither the interest nor the right to remain. Like the population that once squatted in the Ministry of Defense, no one I spoke to at LBS suggested they had any legitimate claim to the space. Once they had been properly compensated, Martin said, they would decamp to the up-country towns and villages from which most of them had

LBS #1

fled during the war. They preferred to make their lives elsewhere and leave the LBS behind.

Liberia's national broadcasting service, the parastatal for which the building was intended, is not likely to reclaim the LBS building as its headquarters. The service has newer accommodations elsewhere in the city. Tearing the building down seems unlikely; LBS is structurally sound, the land on which it sits not especially valuable, and the cost of demolition high. In the near future, then, LBS will likely stand empty. It will be a peculiar relic with a complex history. Like so many of the city's other built forms, it will stand underutilized in a city with massive infrastructure needs.

In his 2013 introduction to an exhibition of recent projects and writings on Africa's built environment, Andres Lepik argues that what the continent needs and what it currently lacks is a suitable African architecture. In rapidly expanding African cities, crumbling modernist infrastructure risks being replaced by a generic "new town" built environment, a proliferation of banal forms that respond in no way to local contexts, needs, or desires (Lepik 2013: 13; see also Uduku 2006). Development funds from the Chinese government and a flood of cash from the petroleum and other resource trades have underwritten massive building campaigns. But the result is expanses of featureless box housing for an as-yet nonexistent middle class. In other cities, whole neighborhoods of generic glass and steel skyscrapers are planned, though few of them may actually be built (see also de Boeck 2011). "The most urgent current priority," writes Lepik in response, "if future African architecture is to discover its own identity . . . [is] high quality reference buildings" (2013: 13).

Lepik's "future African architecture" can, and should, be understood as more than a call for a fashionable building style incorporating African motifs. It could be a vision of the built environment as a productive force in shaping a more equitable postcolonial city. But Lepik's call to frame a future African architecture around a body of high quality reference buildings is more complicated, and potentially more controversial, than it might appear. At very least it creates an interesting tension when read against other ways to imagine the built future of African cities. In what follows, I take up two such visions and propose a third.

The first of these was voiced indirectly by an ex-combatant named Ibrahim as we toured the LBS. For Ibrahim, an African architecture had little to do with form, and everything to do with power. The built environment mattered only to the extent that it could become a tool for the exercise of sovereignty and the generation of profit, which for Ibrahim amounted to essentially the same thing. His vision of African architecture was not one of high-quality reference buildings but of the political might to create and control space.

A future African architecture inspired by the writings on minor architecture represents an opposite vision. Here built forms become revolutionary tools for the disruption of authoritarian state power. Minor architecture offers a vision of an urban future in which the city itself works against the kinds of authority envisioned by Ibrahim as he stood within the LBS. This, too, is an architecture of power, but one that is deconstructed from below.

Both of these are utopian imaginings of what an African architecture might achieve in the continent's cities. They are utopian in the sense David Harvey used the term when he described the sweeping vision of many of the early modern movement designers and planners: "an intense imaginary of some alternative world (both physical and social)" (2000: 164). Like most utopian visions, they do their work by erasing the history of the city and its material realities. As imaginaries of alternative worlds, they would build the new African architecture without confronting and contending with the ruins of the city as found, the ruins on which the population of Monrovia struggles to live, and to thrive, now.

But Lepik's call for a new African architecture founded on high-quality reference buildings suggests a third alternative. No less utopian than the other two, it is, however, a strategy for architectural intervention that does not rely on the erasure of history or the built forms that history has generated on the urban landscape. Realistically for a city like Monrovia, high-quality reference buildings would most easily be realized from the city's existing built forms. And, what is more, they would come from paying careful attention to the history of those forms and the meaning of those structures' original designs. This is, I would argue, the basis of a more radical but realizable future for an African architecture in Monrovia. Its basic elements are already present in a built form like the LBS. Reanimating those architectural moments so that they create locally meaningful connections to global histories seems both a more realistic and ultimately more powerful way to create "Afritecture" than to imagine an African architecture invented sui generis.

LBS #2

LBS #3

Non - existent middle class

The Transparency of Radio

The LBS, like Monrovia's Ministry of Defense, was a product of President Samuel Doe's 1980s *grands projets* approach to modernizing Monrovia. The same Israeli firm designed and constructed the building, and the material resemblance to the exterior of Defense is striking. It, too, is squat and severe, made of block infill on a roughly constructed concrete frame.

The interior of the LBS is therefore something of a surprise. The four sides of the structure surround an interior courtyard that extends from ground floor to ceiling. In the center of the space is a wide, floating stair that connects all three floors. The stair's breadth, supported by a single column, means that anyone ascending or descending the stairwell is visible from the balconies that ring the interior courtyard. Metaphorically, they are suspended in the center of both the horizontal and vertical planes. The surrounding balconies are themselves quite open and visually accessible, however, so the experience of moving through the center of the building is less one of surveillance than of dialogue between the central stair and the surrounding space.

This open atmosphere is reinforced at the ceiling. Although the glazing is gone, a system of thin metal supports spans the ceiling above the courtyard, suggesting a glassed roof and an interior washed in light. The shadows cast by the support system are delicate, and they accentuate, rather than diminish, the light that fills the building's public spaces. For all the militancy of LBS's exterior, its interior is surprisingly, even jarringly, transparent.

It seems a fitting aesthetic for a building that would house the nation's radio service, the primary news source in Liberia as on most of the continent. If, as Benedict Anderson (1991) put it, national media was an essential element in creating the nation as an imagined community, it is radio that has done most of that work in sub-Saharan Africa. President Samuel Doe himself undoubtedly saw his broadcasting service as a propaganda tool, but the designers of the LBS building evidently took seriously the ideal of a national radio network as a public good and a political commons. Though the broadcast system itself had relatively limited reach, the interior of the building that was intended to house it is unusually accessible and transparent in design.

Nostalgia for the Future

Children ran up and down the central stairwell as Martin led me and a small group of companions around the building.[1] Together we wove through the traffic of adults hauling water and firewood to the upper floors. The remaining thin steel supports in the roof dappled the light, giving the entire courtyard a strangely serene atmosphere despite the intense noise, smells, and images of many people living in close proximity. From the strategic placement of catchment buckets and drying laundry, it was possible to map the building's geography of sunlight and moisture. One could clearly see how the building's residents orchestrated their own architecture within the huge frame, carving and creating spaces as they continuously negotiated their needs in relation to the possibilities afforded by the space. Looking down from the stair into the ground floor, pools of standing green water were a reminder of the limits of these creative reworkings. In the torrential Liberian rains, the building's inhabitants are violently exposed to the elements.

"A building like this should be productive," muttered Ibrahim, a young man who had accompanied me on similar explorations of the Ministry of Defense and the E. J. Roye Building, during which he had said almost exactly the same thing. It had become for him a kind of mantra repeated in all of the city's ruins.

As I pressed him about this later, it was clear that his vision of what would make the LBS productive did not include the everyday urbanisms of the LBS residents themselves. "If you leave a building like this to the people," he said, "it will rot and become useless." His was a view diametrically opposed to some of the most progressive literature in architecture, a literature that seeks to validate occupations like those of the LBS Residents' Association and to make it the model for new grassroots forms of architecture and urbanism. In this literature it is the work of squatters and other organic intellectuals that is the most productive. Only the unplanned ruin spaces of the city can truly be generative (see, for example, Koolhaas 2002; Solnit 2005: 90, cited in La Cecla 2012: 14). By contrast, Ibrahim asserted that what Monrovia needed was someone who could lay claim to the built forms of the city from above, not below.

In early 2012 this was not mere fantasy. The verdict in former Liberian president Charles Taylor's trial was read out on April 26, not long after my last visit to LBS. Taylor was indicted for war crimes by the Special Court for Sierra

LBS #4

LBS #5

Leone, and for four years his case was argued in the Hague. Found guilty on eleven counts for his involvement in the fighting across the border, Taylor was sentenced to fifty years in prison.

It was not hard to start a conversation among Monrovians about the Taylor trial, though it was somewhat overshadowed by the Chelsea versus Barcelona match in the UEFA Champions League soccer semifinal. Unlikely as it seemed, there was a strong sense that Taylor might be found not guilty or might escape and return to Liberia. He was a survivor, a powerful man capable of virtually anything. And if he returned, I was told again and again, he would be welcomed. Even young men who fought against Taylor in the 1990s and early 2000s argued that though President Ellen Johnson Sirleaf was doing her best, Liberia needed a strong leader if the situation were to improve for young people in the country. And Charles Taylor was certainly that.

Taylor's election in 1996 was a mystery to outside observers. But for many Liberians, Taylor, feared as he was, had demonstrated that he understood and could control state power (see Ellis 1999; Hoffman 2006; Moran 2006: 101–123). Taylor was ruthless and ruled Liberia as a personal fiefdom, but there was no question that he was deeply engaged with virtually every aspect of daily life in Monrovia. Taylor's various security services were secretive, capricious, and seemingly omnipresent. Their brand of justice was severe. And Taylor's vast and complex web of business enterprises meant that he profited from all manner of commercial transactions in the city, large and small. But for many young people looking back at the Taylor presidency, Monrovia's violence and even its poverty had a kind of coherence missing in the post-Taylor era. Compared to Monrovia in 2012, as one young man put it succinctly, "We lived a better life during the Taylor years." "We don't need a weak man," another ex-combatant told me, not long after Taylor left the country and the perception of a city in chaos had begun to grow. "You need someone who can say, 'I want this cleaned up!' Taylor was the right president for Liberians."

The logic seemed more or less the same across the city and across a diversity of populations. Petty crime had been less under Taylor than it was at the moment. Money flowed more freely, even if it was channeled through Taylor's patronage networks. Corruption was bad of course but today it was worse. And, even more significantly, it was a corruption that siphoned money and resources out of the country. At least Taylor's commitment to Liberia was never in doubt. According to Koffi, the commander in the Zimbabwe neighborhood, for the country's elites today, "Liberia is just a farm. You come here to hustle, get what you can get, go back to America, and live your life. Ellen [Johnson Sirleaf] is educated, but the people around her don't have the country at heart. Ellen will not even live in Liberia after her presidency. She will go back to America. She doesn't even have a house here."

Again and again in conversations in the ruins of the LBS, as in the Ministry of Defense or in the shadow of the E. J. Roye tower, there was a striking "nostalgia for the future," as Piot (2010) calls it—a longing for a moment in which it was possible to plan a future in West Africa, a project that for many young people seems difficult, even impossible, today. And for most of those ex-combatant Monrovians with whom I spoke, one of the preconditions for such a future was a patriarchal political figure who could establish and wield authoritarian control. The absence of a strong man had not yielded a more benevolent, participatory, or democratic state. It had produced a more crushing form of authoritarianism in the form of extreme uncertainty. "When I look at democracy, and the rule of law," said a young ex-combatant named Amarie, who fought first for Taylor and then against him on behalf of LURD, "if you have democracy and you don't have the rule of law, you don't have a real democracy." Taylor's law could be arbitrary but there was no doubting its existence.

Ibrahim's observation that a building like the LBS should be productive has therefore to be seen in the context of this unfolding conversation about the possible return of Taylor and, by extension, the nature of the political imaginary in Liberia in early 2012. The quotidian activities of the urban populace were not, by themselves, productive. They were a means of survival and nothing more. Certainly Ibrahim and the other ex-combatants with whom I spoke could not see in the occupation of the LBS or the other ruins of the city the potential for anything other than continued precarity. They could never be more.

What would be productive would be a figure powerful enough to reclaim spaces like the LBS and make it part of his personalized network of political, economic, and social patronage. Exactly what Taylor might do with a building like LBS was left unspecified. But there was no question that he could, and would, instigate sweeping changes to the city—as indeed he did in successive rounds of urban warfare throughout the 1990s and early 2000s, and as he did throughout his presidency. He would bring back to Monrovia "an intense

LBS #7

FACING PAGE: *LBS #6*

imaginary of an alternative world." He would be able to make the ruins of the city productive again.

Ibrahim's vision of a future African architecture under a sovereign authority like Taylor included no formal or material dimensions because it was a completely monetized vision. "In Africa," he said at one point in our conversation about a possible Taylor return, politics is simply "the fastest, and the safest, way to make money." Understood as such, the built components of state and parastate functions are largely irrelevant, because public life does not require it. What matters a great deal more is the spectacular appearance of wealth and the ability to distribute that wealth along personalized networks of patronage. As de Boeck has written of contemporary Kinshasa, the actual materialization of built forms is not what this kind of "ocular" urbanism is about. What matters is the ability to formulate a fantastic of vision of what the city could be, a vision outrageous, perhaps impossible, enough to eclipse reality and become the daydream even of those most marginalized by the flows of wealth through the metropolis (de Boeck 2011: 272–280).

This stands in marked contrast to an earlier moment in which the ability to realize modern forms was the index of sovereignty and nationhood in postcolonial Africa. In Ghana, for example, Janet Hess (2000) has described how the capacity to generate projects in the international style served the dual purpose of enshrining the Nkrumah administration and symbolically unifying the modern nation (see also Larkin 2008). Significantly, the projects Hess catalogs as part of this inventory of architectural modernism are heavily weighted toward public buildings and spaces: the State House, Black Star Square, and the National Museum, for example.

Fifty years later, Ibrahim's version of a future African architecture manifested in the LBS made no space for a public sphere or national symbolism. It therefore had no aesthetic requirements for the built forms that would house such public entities as a national broadcasting service. Taylor exercised sovereignty through rumor and "vulgar" aesthetics (Mbembe 1992), through disembodied and ephemeral spectacles of power, not the more place-based forms of governance through public dialogue or debate.

Ibrahim's utopian vision of the future Monrovia was, in short, a vision of African urbanism but not a vision of the city. It was "an intense imaginary of an alternative world" in which the city's forms would facilitate the smooth functioning of the cash nexus: an evaluation of all social, political, and economic relationships as relations of capital (Deleuze and Guattari 1983: 222–261; see also Mbembe 2003, 2006). A building like LBS would be productive when it helped to make the flow of money more efficient and the generation of profit more fluid, something a sovereign like Taylor would know how to do. The city as a political space of agonistic negotiation, a space that would have certain formal requirements and certain aesthetic dimensions, had no place in this imagination of a future African architecture.

Minor Architecture

Ibrahim's future African architecture stands in marked contrast to another possible vision of Monrovia's future.

For a small number of architects and architectural theorists, the enigmatic French philosophers Gilles Deleuze and Félix Guattari represent a radical set of possibilities for rethinking space and design. For most the key text is Deleuze's (1992) *The Fold*, a short commentary on Leibniz and the baroque that has inspired a body of dense theoretical commentary and a few self-consciously Deleuzian structures made up mostly of curving lines.[2]

A second Deleuze and Guattari (1986) text on the writer Franz Kafka has produced a mostly theoretical but more explicitly political body of work. A "minor literature" like Kafka's was, for Deleuze and Guattari, writing that reworked the codes of a "major" language. In contrast to the canonical literatures of the world's colonial or hegemonic languages, they argue, minor literatures find and exploit the points at which language can be put to work otherwise. The goal is new ways of thinking and, ultimately, of living. A minor literature does not eschew the major language but finds ways to inhabit it differently. In Deleuze and Guattari's terms, using Kafka as their main example, minor literatures "deterritorialize" the master language. The result, as Jana Evans Braziel (n.d.) puts it, is always "political, collective, revolutionary, and even spatial—deterritorializing one terrain as it maps another."

The appeal for progressive architects and theorists is obvious. A minor architecture seems in many ways the polar opposite of the avant-garde, social engineering projects of modern movement architecture and much of what came after it. Rather than replacing Le Corbusier's master plans and master narratives with a completely different but equally totalizing design, a Deleuzian minor architecture would presumably offer strategies for deconstructing those grand plans and putting them to new use. It is an approach to the built

LBS #9

FACING PAGE: *LBS #8*

LBS #10

environment that would seem much more in keeping with architecture and urban design's more progressive calls for sustainability, adaptive reuse, participatory design, and collaboration.

Jill Stoner's (2012) *Toward a Minor Architecture* nicely captures the spirit of the minor architecture movement. Where the international style promised beauty and uplift through constructing exquisite, timeless forms, minor architecture is built by taking things apart. In Stoner's reading, architecture is minor when it, like a minor literature, is "political because it is mobilized from below" (2012: 4) and deliberately works to undo relationships of exclusion and power embedded in dominant architectures (6–7). It achieves this largely by dematerializing space, by making the fixed forms of architecture malleable, even irrelevant: "They [minor architectures] will be necessarily ephemeral, slip through cracks of Euclidean convention, and pay no heed to the idea of the formal. Form will tend to dissipate; material will give way to immaterial" (2–3).

Thus the Torre David tower in Caracas is a minor architecture because it is a "half finished corporate tower" that has been "taken hostage as vertical *favela*" (1). Given its almost parasitic nature, minor architecture is best done in the ruins of modern architecture, creating experimental, temporary, and often invisible spaces of invention from the detritus of what is already there.

In Stoner's formulation, much of what makes a minor architecture political is the way it erodes the boundary between the public and the private. Following Deleuze and Guattari, she argues that the state imposes lines between public and private and actively works to maintain them as a way to control what kinds of politics are possible, for whom and when (Stoner 2012: 9). As the physical structure of major built forms is dematerialized, so too is the metaphorical wall that separates the public domain of the political from the private domain of the domestic. Drawing, among other examples, on Benjamin's writings on the crowded tenements of Naples, Stoner describes how a minor architecture refuses to be neatly cataloged into spaces reserved for domesticity and public life. For Benjamin, looking at the seeming chaos of Naples, "the idea of public space in the tradition of the large piazza," she writes, "is replaced by an informal honeycomb of fine-grained interstices—staircases, doorways, balconies, halls, porches, and narrow streets—in which layers of urban and domestic territories blur not only the physical condition of the craggy city but its social stratification as well" (Stoner 2012: 36).

Stoner quotes Benjamin directly as he describes the "porosity" of the Neopolitan (minor) architecture, a deliberate refusal on the part of its inhabitants to restrict their own capacity to experiment, their "passion for improvisation, which demands that space and opportunity be at any price preserved" (Benjamin 1978a, cited in Stoner 2012: 36). In an urban milieu in which spaces are not clearly demarcated along the lines of public and private, every space, and every activity, is potentially public in ways not necessarily sanctioned by the state. Any space can therefore become a space for making political demands, negotiating differences or enacting an agonistic kind of democracy.

Benjamin's description of the urban landscape of Naples, the description Stoner evokes so powerfully as an exemplar of minor architecture, could just as easily have been taken from de Boeck's description of modern Kinshasa, the novelist Chris Abani's (2005) accounts of Lagos, or the Abidjan photographs of Dorris Kasco or Ananias Leki Dago (Dago and Le Goff 2003; Kasco and Deberre 1994). Or they could have come from virtually anywhere in contemporary Monrovia. In this dematerialized urbanity, a clear demarcation between public and private seems impossible to locate. Indeed it seems somewhat absurd. *Private* is not really a term of space in an African urban context defined by lack, improvisation, and (to use Benjamin's word) porosity. A different, more ephemeral and fragmentary demarcation of space seems to characterize most African cities.

As de Boeck puts it: "Everyday lives in Africa's cities are to a large extent conceived around architectures that remain almost invisible and are defined by lack and absence. . . . As such, urban residents are constantly confronted with infrastructural shortcomings and impossibilities, but paradoxically, these in turn also generate new possibilities and opportunities, as well as different kinds of space" (de Boeck 2013: 95; see also Njami 2001; Simone 2004). But de Boeck's description of how the public-private dichotomy is disrupted in Kinshasa sounds a cautionary note. A pervasive consequence of spaces that cannot be clearly demarcated is a kind of genericness to the city. This is true not only of its half-built, constantly morphing physical forms, but also of the kinds of political subjectivities that emerge in those spaces. The same forces that allow, and in fact force, the city's residents to experiment with new ways of living also limit their ability to form a political bloc or articulate collective demands. Physically, socially, and politically, there are few spaces in the city in which collectivities can gather and form. "The possibility of an Arab Spring still seems very remote and unlikely in Africa south of the Sahara," writes de Boeck (2013: 102), because the dialectics of public and private offers no truly private spaces in which a collective political identity can be worked out and no truly public spaces in which to present that identity as a challenge to power (see also Mbembe and Roitman 1995).

There is, in short, an optimism in much of the minor architecture literature that is not necessarily reflected in the reality of those urban spaces where most architecture could be said to already operate in a minor key. Although Stoner (2012: 9) is careful to point out that spaces designed to be public are not automatically democratic spaces, disrupting the public-private distinction appears in her manifesto as an inherently revolutionary act. And yet the absence of this distinction in any meaningful or locatable sense has helped to produce the depoliticized (or even antipolitical [Ferguson 1990]) mode of urbanism that characterizes African cities today. The outsourcing of government functions to NGOs who relate to African populations as statistics and aggregate life processes rather than as citizens; the farce of elections that produce brokered unity governments regardless of vote tallies; the arbitrary fees imposed for the performance of public services like policing, schooling, or identification all speak to an erosion of the idea of the public in a way that has not generated a more equitable city or a new egalitarian politics. As Patrick Bond (2006) puts it, a state capable of imposing such rigid and predictable classifications between public and private is seen by many in Africa not as a problem but as a potential (if unlikely) solution.

In short, the kinds of minor architecture that are already being enacted around the city have done nothing to erase or even erode the exclusions that characterize the operation of power in the city. Nor are they likely to. They have without doubt produced spaces of invention and improvisation. But unlike the Torre David tower in Caracas or any of the real or fictive spaces in which one finds minor architectures (or insurgent practices of architecture or citizenship [see Holston 2008; Hou 2010]), the practices of innovation in the LBS or Monrovia's other ruins have failed to generate a meaningful political identity for those forced to practice it.

Architecture of Openness

Writing in the early 1960s, as many African states were gaining or fighting for independence, the architectural historian Udo Kultermann (1963, 1969) argued that architecture would matter to the nations of the continent when a distinctly African architecture emerged. Such an architecture, he argued, would be firmly grounded in vernacular building traditions and would address local aspirations and needs.

Half a century later, Lepik (2013) argues that this call remains largely unanswered. African architecture still has no identity. In the Kultermann tradition, Lepik suggests that this is largely because there have been few projects on the continent that successfully combine meaningful vernacular building traditions, address pressing social needs, and represent "beautiful form" (2013: 18). Those rare built projects that might constitute the beginnings of a canon are largely unknown outside a small circle of specialists (13–14).[3]

Lepik's story of how a distinct architecture emerges is a conventional one within architectural history: an African architecture, like any architectural school or approach, would develop from a recognizable body of work to which future designers would respond. These high-quality reference buildings would become the foundation for a complex but coherent movement. As in any utopian plan, Lepik's vision largely erases the complexities of history as experienced in most African cities, Monrovia included. Just like Ibrahim's vision of an architecture made productive by the return of Taylor or another neopatrimonial strongman, and like minor architecture's imaginary of an entirely deconstructive, grassroots occupation of space, Lepik's vision of the built form of the city largely begins with a tabula rasa.

Given the current state of much of the continent's modernist built form, and given its strong association with a history of colonialism and repression, Lepik argues, the architecture of the last hundred years has little or no place in that evolution. This phase of history and the built environment must be erased in the course of building more equitable cities. The challenge moving forward is to replace what exists now with new forms, forms that combine vernacular architectures with modern technology and environmental sensibilities.

In fact, the ruins of the modernist era in Monrovia have never been viewed by most Monrovians as simple artifacts of an exploitative past that should be forgotten or wished away.[4] The patrimony of modernist built forms includes most of the national administrative buildings, one of the largest and most sophisticated hospitals in West Africa, a well-regarded university campus, and two world-class hotels, at least some of them designed by Liberian architects. For many Monrovians, modernity is something from which they feel excluded today by the inequities of the global economy (see Ferguson 1999, 2006), but the city's modernist ruins are a reminder not of past oppression but of a moment in which it was possible to believe in the forward march of progress and to imagine a cosmopolitan future.

In other words, accepting that Lepik is correct and that a future African architecture could be established on the foundations of a body of high-quality reference buildings, there is no reason why the existing built infrastructure of the city cannot and should not form a significant element in that movement's core. Indeed, it seems more realistic that a city like Monrovia would adapt and reuse its existing forms than invent them anew. But to do so means working with the material at hand, both the physical forms of these ruins and the social and political meanings they express. It means taking seriously the poetics of these structures, their histories, and their latent meanings. In some cases, such as the Ministry of Defense, such a reclamation might be impossible. Both the form and history of the building are too saturated with meaning ever to be put to use otherwise. But the LBS, it seems, is different. Its latent possibilities are more open to a different set of claims.

THE ELEMENTS THAT GIVE THE LBS its air of openness have a peculiar pedigree. The two most striking features, the flying stairwell and the transparent ceiling, are both traceable to architectural innovations that were intended to express, and to enhance, the changing nature of work in the modern era.

Take the design of the central stair. In one of the most famous early modern movement projects, the Fagus shoe-last factory in Germany (1911–1913), Walter Gropius and Adolf Meyer set out to create an image of "pure economic rationality" (Cohen 2012: 85). Gropius and Meyer were at the time part of a cadre of architects pushing factory design away from structures that looked and felt like heavy industrial fortresses and toward large production spaces that were light-filled, flexible, and efficient.[5] The goal was a structure with the clear logic and machinelike precision of modern industry. For Gropius and Meyer, therefore, the odd mandate for the Fagus Factory was especially providential: to take an existing, conventional factory plan from another architect and rework its exterior elements so that the building, especially as it would appear from passing trains, would create "an image of arresting modernity" (Darley 2003: 143; see also Banham 1989: 181–194).

Gropius and Meyers responded by dematerializing parts of the building in a few radical design moves. Where traditionally the two walls of a large building would meet at a structurally significant, heavy joint, Gropius and Meyer put glass, cantilevered to give the impression of being unsupported. A stairwell immediately behind the glass therefore appears to be free floating within a transparent case. The result celebrates movement as the factory's core logic. Circulation itself seems to hold the building up and keep everything in place.

One way to read the Fagus Factory innovations is as an effort to demystify the inner workings of the factory. Visually its design elements broadcast the connections between Fordist production methods and the wider networks of transportation and communication that make those methods possible. The Fagus Factory corner was, in short, a clever piece of engineering that symbolically linked modern networks of factory production to the networks that made the nation itself modern.

The LBS, like many other structures built after Fagus, repeats the logic of the precedent. It takes a normally hidden service element (the stairwell) and celebrates it as the most visible expression of the building's *parti*.[6] A conversation between multiple interlocutors, and the possibilities of dialogue born out of movement, are the organizing principles expressed by the relatively simple design. Located at the center of the structure and visible from all sides, the space elevates this open conversation to a central theme.

The transparency of the LBS's core is repeated by the thinness of the roof of the building, which seemed to draw its inspiration from a second thread in the modernist architectural canon. Where the Fagus Factory used glass to make a statement about European industrial production, Frank Lloyd Wright's Larkin Building (1902–1906), the administrative headquarters of the Larkin soap factory in Buffalo, New York, uses it to underscore the role of capital and finance in early twentieth-century America.

From the outside, the Larkin Building was a solid mass of thick brick walls and sharply rectangular towers.[7] The heavy massing of the walls, however, surrounded an interior courtyard that extended all the way up through the building to a thin glass ceiling. At the ground floor, under what was essentially a massive skylight, the Larkin company's clerks worked at row after row of desks in an open floor plan that was novel for the time (Cohen 2012: 63). Form, light, and function were integrated to enable, and to celebrate, the smooth operation of ever more complex and expanding commercial networks.

The glass and steel technology that made the space possible was relatively new, and the result was a space that equated innovations in the organization of work with innovations in structural engineering. Both signified modernity and the modern economy.

If the meaning in modern architecture lies in its tectonics, the way it marries the dichotomy between earth and sky, the labor of support, and the ephemerality of enclosure (Frampton 1990: 521; see also Frascari 1984), then the Larkin Building unabashedly privileged the celestial and equated it with the quantitative side of mass industrial production. Removing the barrier between the work of managers and the sky, the Larkin was a building that celebrated the labor of numbers by making that labor as open as possible. The design facilitated efficient, and potentially limitless, connections enabled by ever-expanding material and immaterial networks. Wright put that connective work in the open and imposed upon it as few restrictions as possible, emphasizing materially and symbolically the increasing importance of large bureaucratized corporations in American social, political, and economic life.

Neither the Fagus Factory nor the Larkin Building express a radical politics. In fact, seen from the postmodern present, both appear deeply conservative and uncritical. But both Gropius and Wright were involved throughout their careers in efforts to use architecture as a tool for progressive social ends (see, for example, Cohen 2012: 228, 292). Both are of a piece with the progressive, high-modernist ideal that mass production would lead to improved standards of living for workers. They are utopian projects in that sense, incorporating elements that expressed the sweeping changes of their period and working to enshrine the new social, political, and economic landscape in built form.

At very least, the work Gropius, Meyers, and Wright did on these two structures expresses an ethical stance toward demystifying the economic and social processes they enable and house. There is no reason why finding ways to recuperate these poetics should not be part of a project of developing a new African architectural identity. The real question is whether or not the ethics of demystification that inspired these designs can be built upon. Could they become part of a vocabulary that informs a future African architecture, capturing some of the currents of nationalism, optimism, and public commons that are poetically expressed by the original design? Why should these not be reference elements in a distinctly "aftermodern" (Enwezor 2010) African built form?

The Possibility of an Insurgent Architecture

Standing on the third floor of the LBS under the open sky, an older man named Michael was waving his hands like an orchestra conductor. From where we stood, it was possible to see three-quarters of the building. Michael was mapping the visible spaces with his hands, pointing out which families lived where, how the rooms had been divided, what areas were uninhabitable or could be used only when there was no rain.

Michael held a small key tucked under his thumb, a ubiquitous everyday artifact in Monrovia. The Chinese or Nigerian padlock to which it belonged would mark a boundary, reserving the contents of a suitcase, trunk, or room for Michael and whoever held the second key. It was a small but elegant symbol of domesticity set against the vast expanse of the LBS. Somehow it highlighted the tragedy and absurdity of Michael's situation. He was a long-term transient in a building never intended for the purpose to which it had been put. He and hundreds of other squatters had established a place for themselves in the LBS, mostly through creative and bold improvisation. But it was hard to read their presence as anything other than a precarious response to an impossible situation. Surveying the ruins of the LBS as Michael narrated the building, neither the sweeping top-down authoritarianism of a Charles Taylor–like sovereign nor a minor architecture swelling up from below seemed capable of addressing the profound needs of the LBS residents.

Clearly the issues that face Michael and other Monrovians today are large-scale, structural ones. But as the anthropologist Franco La Cecla (2012: 14–16) argues, it is disingenuous to assume that small-scale architectural interventions are purely aesthetic, divorced from the politics of the city writ large. Design decisions are inevitably part of the larger machinery that shapes the city as a whole, and a truly "insurgent architecture" (Harvey 2000: 206) is composed of interventions at multiple scales. Imagining that simple elements like the cast of a stair or the structure of a roof could become part of a lexicon of habitation in a more equitable form of African urbanism is clearly utopian. But in that, it is no more utopian than its alternatives.

PHOTOGRAPHIC POSTSCRIPT

A handful of modern and contemporary architects — Le Corbusier, Steven Holl, Carlo Scarpa — are known for their treatment of light. Quality of light is clearly a central concern for any photographer, but architectural photography that treats

LBS #3

LBS #5

LBS #6

LBS #8

LBS #9

the quality and fall of light as an ethnographic fact is more rare. Guido Guidi's (2011) long-term documentation of Scarpa's Tomba Brion is, among other things, an investigation of Scarpa's use of light to make the space meaningful, and the result is a remarkably anthropological book: an entirely depopulated account of the importance of light and form in religious iconography and imagination.

In the photographs that make up the visual elements in the LBS photo-essay, quality of light becomes an ethnographic issue. The argument that a structure like the LBS could become part of a canon of meaningful African architecture requires some counterargument to the presumption, common not only in architectural circles but in the popular imagination, that modernism was only ever a form violently imposed on the African landscape. *LBS #6* explores the play of light on form as an alternative. Here the harshness and surreality of the vast incompleteness of the space is rendered more humane by the play of light and shadow on the exposed surfaces. There is in the way the light is cast in the building the possibility of a different meaning. It is the visual evidence that in the building's design and construction there was originally a more utopian aspiration, something that spoke to a meaningful architecture that could be about more than the imposition of power, à la the Ministry of Defense. *LBS #6* is thus an image that uses the play of light as structured by the architecture to ask whether other, recoverable possibilities are inherent in the form itself, possibilities that do not have to be read as somehow inauthentic to the African city in which the building is located. It is an argument more subtly repeated in *LBS #8* and *LBS #9*. Both are banal, quotidian scenes. The surrounding architecture is present in the images, but the real subject in both images is light. In each case it is a soft luminescence. By comparison to the harsh glare that penetrates the E. J. Roye in many of those photographs, a light that emphasizes the building's ruined state, in the LBS light becomes one of the tools of domesticity. The images make an argument that the building can be more meaningfully occupied because its relation to the elements is cooperative, intentionally or unintentionally scaled and modulated at a pitch that allows for life to happen in a way that is manageable for those living it within the building's walls.

The manageability of the architecture of the LBS is underscored in other ways in the images. Both *LBS #3* and *LBS #5* are, at first read, ambiguous. The ground under the young girl clinging to the exterior column is only barely discernible. It is hard, without careful inspection, to know whether falling from her precarious place on the wall would be fatal or fun. Similarly, the tiny key hung from a finger in *LBS #5* could point to an absurdity, the desperate futility of trying to secure anything in a space without doors or complete walls.

And yet in both images that ambiguity can also point toward a more optimistic reading of the photographs and the spaces they depict. In the context of the images that surround them, these photographs make gestures toward normalcy in an otherwise abnormal space. The girl's movements across the building's façade are clearly a form of play rather an act of desperation. It would be too easy and too unobservant to see the photograph simply as a metaphor for the precarity of life in the ruins of a postwar city — not when presented in conjunction with the images of a functional, albeit impoverished, form of existence elsewhere in the building. The key as a visual icon similarly points to the fact that somewhere in the building exists something on a scale and in a state such that it can be meaningfully protected, something that warrants being demarcated as private. Again, to see this image as one of a series of images that documents the domestication of a space is to see in it a more optimistic argument for the possibilities for living that the space affords.

CHAPTER 6

Finding Urban Form
A Coda

South African photographer Guy Tillim's series of projects from around sub-Saharan Africa is, perhaps, the best-known work on the continent's modernist ruins (see, e.g., Tillim 2005, 2009). His largely depopulated images work as nested frames: the camera frames once-luxury office towers, bureaucratic offices, and massive urban infrastructure projects as they, in turn, frame evidence of the lives of those who move through them. Doors and windows are a recurrent trope, underscoring the thematics of passage in space and time. "How strange that modernism," Tillim (2009) writes in the preface to *Avenue Patrice Lumumba*, "which eschewed monument and past for nature and future should carry such memory so well." The memory that interests Tillim is utopian memory. It is memory of the promises of independence in Africa and the haunting death of those dreams. His photographs are architectural photographs, but they document how lives are lived in that postutopian dreamscape.

Tillim, critic and theorist Okwui Enwezor argues, explores ways of being in the African city that are not, however, about failure or the missteps of history. They are, rather, about the possibilities for inventing the future: "His [Tillim's] photographic project is an expression of hope that showing the decaying legacy of colonial modernity in Africa is not an attempt to mourn the loss of some great past but a possible tabula rasa for future cosmopolitanism" (Enwezor 2010: 616). It is a curious characterization, given that it seems to run counter to Tillim's own description of his work. While Tillim claims his images are not a "mediation on aspects of late-modernist era colonial situations," he does find real meaning in the material forms of the structures that period produced. These buildings, he writes, are an active presence "struggling to contain the calamities of the past fifty years." It is certainly true that Tillim is using the camera to understand what "indisputably African identity" is being created within these spaces. But what the resulting images express is that this process does not occur in a vacuum or on a blank canvas. It is inextricably bound to the particularities of the built environment.

The dichotomy implicit in Enwezor's characterization of Tillim's work is one that runs through both the literature on ruins and much of the literature of African urbanism today. The city image (both the photograph of the city and the city as itself an image) is either a signifier of postcolonial degradation or a blank slate on which to project hopeful imaginings of the future. In ruin, the built form is either a site of mourning or a site of hope. Either way, however, the built environment is no longer active architectural space. It is simply a backdrop, passive and silent.

Tillim's images invite a different reading: the disorienting cylinder of Johannesburg's Ponte City apartment tower; the monumentalism of the Grande Hotel in Beira, Mozambique; the absurdity of dismembered and discarded statues that commemorate the dramatic rise and fall of colonial and postcolonial sovereigns; concrete walls that melt and mold in the moist tropical heat. These are not blank spaces. Their materiality is palpable in the images. Their scale and texture, their tone and meaning are attributes with which the people who move through them must contend. Reading these structures as forces or actors in the city, the urban "aftermodern" becomes something different: a complex landscape in which built form and political imagination remain in tension and in dialogue, acting one upon the other.

In the chapters of this book, I have similarly sought to trace the ordering work done by material forms. For the most part I have emphasized how that ordering forecloses some urban futures, how it makes imagining some ways to be in the city impossible. If a city's residents, as Heidegger (1993: 363) argued, "must ever learn to dwell," Monrovia's modernism makes some kinds of learning, and some kinds of dwelling, impossible. To explore these spaces, I have relied on the camera as a research tool, and photography as a communicative medium, working alongside the text to photowrite built forms. Word and image together are central to the project just as they are central to how modernist architectural spaces came into being.

Ultimately, then, this too is a story about how lives are lived in an African city today. While in this book I have mostly told that story through four buildings, it is a story repeated spatially and temporally throughout the city, often away from the camera though, occasionally, spectacularly before it. I conclude with one such moment. My coda occurred after the fieldwork for the rest of this project was complete. It is architectural to the extent that it, like the built environment at the heart of *Monrovia Modern*, is ultimately about the sociopolitics of how space is defined and form imposed in an African urban environment. If "it is the work of form to make order," as Levine puts it, "and this means that forms are the stuff of politics" (2015: 6; see also Grosz 2001: 154–155), then the formal arrangements of architecture must be legible elsewhere on the political landscape of the city. The themes and analytics I have used to explore these particular places, my "thick section" (Way 2013) of those four spaces, should be recognizable outside them—outside, even, of architectural spaces in an orthodox sense. In one of the most devastating moments in Monrovia's difficult history, the 2014–2015 outbreak of Ebola virus disease, they were.

"WE ARE DYING. THE whole city is dying." It was a disturbing call, not least because I knew Jowee as a man not given to panic or hyberbole. A veteran of Charles Taylor's Small Boys Unit, he had seen, indeed been a participant in, Monrovia's darkest moments since the early 1990s. His voice broke momentarily, then he went on: "Liberia is hell. People are scared. They don't know what's going on. You don't go see your family. The border is closed. The Guinea border is closed. The Sierra Leone border is closed. Everything is closed. Nothing going out. Nothing coming in. We are drowning." Jowee detailed all the places that the 2014–2015 outbreak of Ebola virus disease (or simply Ebola) in Monrovia had made it impossible to travel. He couldn't leave the city for the village, where only a handful of his extended family still lived, but in which a wide network of kin gathered in times of crisis, death, or celebration. He couldn't cross town to see his sister or her husband, a former militia commander to whom he still appealed as a patron in difficult moments. He couldn't hustle, couldn't travel the city streets to look for odd jobs, beg favors, or collect on debts. Jowee, like much of Monrovia, was stuck.

The twenty-four-month Ebola epidemic is estimated to have killed over 11,300 people in Sierra Leone, Liberia, and Guinea, as well as a handful of others across West Africa, Europe, and the United States. Though it has periodically flared in different parts of the continent since at least the mid-1970s, in its scale and severity this was the disease's most intense manifestation. This was also the first time that Ebola had become an urban problem. In the absence of a chemical prophylactic or much understanding of the epidemiology of the disease, the physical isolation of parts of the population was one of the principal weapons deployed for combating Ebola in Monrovia and elsewhere.

Quarantine, the spatial containment of groups of people who were not necessarily Ebola carriers but who were perceived to be either risky or at risk, was the bluntest but also one of the most widely employed tools against the disease. Especially in the early days of the crisis, mass isolation through quarantines and cordons sanitaires seemed to many to be the only effective response to a contagion that some projections estimated could kill hundreds of thousands or millions of people.

The encircling, spherical form of the quarantines was, like any form, a political ordering. As such, quarantines had material and immaterial dimensions. They were discursive constructs as well as physical ones. The quarantine was both a concrete intervention against Ebola and a sociopolitical fantasy that gave the disease meaning.

The most dramatic and draconian quarantine occurred when, on the morning of August 20, Liberian security personnel moved into the West Point slum and attempted to implement a complete cordon sanitaire. Troops placed barricades of razor wire, wooden pallets, market tables, and vehicles around the neighborhood. Armed police and soldiers stood on the far side of the circle, and announcements went out that the quarter was under total lockdown. Passage in or out was forbidden, and the security personnel there to enforce the quarantine were armed with live ammunition.

The response by West Point's residents was immediate. Groups of young men rushed the barricades, trying to break through. A fifteen-year-old boy by the name of Shakie Kamara, allegedly not part of the rioting groups, was shot in the legs and left on the street, eventually becoming the one confirmed casualty of security force activity. Traders with foodstuffs doubled and tripled the prices of basic supplies. And, most notoriously, a group of West Point residents did the seemingly unthinkable: they stormed the neighborhood's

Ebola treatment center, turning out infectious patients and looting the facility of highly contagious, fluid-soaked mattresses, blankets, and supplies.

The quarantine spiraled quickly from tragedy to farce. After the initial violence, residents living on the edges of the barricades began finding ways to sneak out windows or through zinc walls of shacks, opening an underground railroad of sorts for which they could charge neighbors to exit and (less often) enter the quarantine zone. Others sought out soldiers who were willing to look the other way for a small fee while residents climbed over, under, or around the blockades. Still others swam out of the neighborhood. Ten days after it was announced, the West Point quarantine was called off, an obvious failure.

Although many commentators claimed that such drastic spatial separation was a medieval tactic that hadn't been a part of the toolkit for combating disease in over a century, the fact is that safeguarding health has been a recurrent theme in colonial discourses of racial separation across Africa.[1] As such, the shape of many, even most, African urban centers has been greatly influenced by measures to quarantine risky populations. The legacy of the space-health nexus is still legible in the highly different character of the various quarters of cities from Algiers to Dakar to Lagos to Cape Town. The imposition of the quarantine in contemporary Monrovia was unusually dramatic and severe, but as a tactic of urban planning in Africa it was not especially rare.

If the West Point quarantine shares a genealogy with urban spatial practices common across colonial African cities, it also bears a family resemblance to the ideals of modernist design writ large. The Cartesian ordering of space that characterized high modernist architecture and urban planning was defined by its alleged universality, by the global applicability of certain fundamentals regardless of social context. Like the elemental geometry of modernist architecture, the quarantine's formal logic is one of seemingly primordial shapes imposed in space. The hermetically sealed sphere is a natural shape of enclosure, of defining and isolating space and its contents.

Imposed under the extreme duress of a raging epidemic, the formal spatial ordering of the quarantine highlighted Monrovians' more complex and less Cartesian understanding of the geography of the city. The very logic of fixing space as a form of security runs counter to a mode of urban habitation common to contemporary African cities, Monrovia included (see chapter 1). The anthropologist Catherine Bolten, responding to Sierra Leone's nationwide quarantine regimen, noted the cognitive dissonance that was obvious to many Sierra Leoneans but largely invisible to many of the international responders. Urged (or in some cases ordered) to stay at home, many Sierra Leoneans envisioned a network of interlinking spaces rather than a single, fixed site.[2] Rural ancestral villages, multiple urban residences, outlying farms, or labor encampments all have valences of home in different times and contexts. So, too, do spaces outside the national borders of the state, as the contemporary African experience is increasingly a transnational one (see D'Alisera 2004; Hepner 2009; MacGaffey and Bazenguissa-Ganga 2000; Maher 2015; Piot 2010; Smith 2015).

It was exactly this multisited meaning of place that Jowee implicitly referenced when he spoke of a city dying because its residents were unable to move. Monrovians were trapped in the city, unable to move within it or beyond it. The injunction to remain restricted in space had implications beyond a simple interdiction against movement. It constituted an affront to what it means to be a modern urban subject. For Jowee, as for many Monrovians (ex-combatants not least among them), the impossibility of movement meant a dead social landscape. Movement and vitality are synonymous, and arresting that movement, as much as the disease epidemic that prompted it, was killing the city.

This was, in other words, a rapidly accelerated but nevertheless consistent instance of the work of political ordering through urban form that is evident at a larger scale and longer time frames, in the constitution of the modern city itself. And it brought into stark relief the set of suppositions and conclusions that I have explored through image and text in these pages. There is no proper way to inhabit the quarantine any more than there is a proper way to inhabit modern architecture or indeed the modern city writ large. Trapped as they were behind militarized barricades with known cases of a poorly understood disease, the residents of West Point found themselves confronted by an urban configuration in which it was not obvious how one might live. They were subject to an urban spatial logic that sought to regulate the flows and exchange of bodies, goods, even information, but which afforded them no recognizable space for political engagement. The fact that the quarantine proved remarkably ineffective in the face of the inventiveness and creativity of those subject to it is, of course, an important part of Monrovia's urban story under Ebola. But so too is the fact that those selfsame practices of subversion and invention included no real claim to any right to life in the city. Those who could fled West Point. Others moved back and forth across the quarantine line, paying their tolls to both cynical officials of the state and their entrepreneurial neighbors. The rights to movement and isolation were cathected onto the logic of the cash flows rather than the rights of citizenship or even the logic of disease vectors and spreading pathogens. And in the most extreme instance, the looting of the Ebola treatment center, the response was a kind of magical realism. Invited by agents of the state security forces to stay put in West Point, those who attacked the Ebola center simply underscored that as residents of the poorest neighborhood in Monrovia, encircled by armed agents of the state, they had no logical and effective way to formulate a call for reconsideration or redress and no one to whom such a call might be addressed. They chose instead an act of nihilism, a utopian fantasy that they could live in a world in which Ebola did not exist.[3]

IN HIS BRIEF INTRODUCTION to Tillim's (2009) *Avenue Patrice Lumumba*, the pioneering ethnographic filmmaker Robert Gardner asks whether it is "the particular genius of photography to indicate, ironically enough by its estimable verisimilitude, crucial aspects of the meaning hidden in actuality." Photography is an especially good medium for exploring hidden meanings in the visible world, and one I have relied on extensively in the preceding pages. I am not sure, however, that its genius is necessarily particular: the same impulse seems inherent to the anthropological project as a whole. The written archives of Monrovia, its history on film, the current aesthetics and practices of everyday urbanism visibly and invisibly unfolding on the city streets—all are sites of hidden meaning, sites of circulating form and therefore of political ordering.

And there is no doubt a good deal of meaning hidden in the modernist ruins of Monrovia, just as there is in the built environment of all African cities; a good deal of matter that matters, to play with Cairns and Jacobs's (2014: 31–32) useful phrasing. Once made visible, by the camera or other means, the project becomes one of tracing those meaningful forms and the political work they do throughout the many other facets of the city: its architecture, its planning, its design, the organization of its economy and politics, its arts, its various crises. This has been my project here. Though they do so in different ways, the four buildings at the heart of *Monrovia Modern* are articulations of an ordering of the political imagination. Those articulations resonate with others across the urban landscape of modern Monrovia, a city subject to the ongoing ruination of history, of war and disease, of the inequities of the global economy. Monrovia's history has been a difficult one. Its future will be as well. Understanding the circulation of its forms, and the political imaginations made possible and foreclosed as a result, is imperative if the city's future residents are to invent for themselves meaningful new ways to dwell.

Notes

Preface

1 According to the UNHCR, at the end of June 2013 the registered Somali population at Dadaab stood at 409,000. By the end of September 2016 the camp population had been reduced to 261,000, and the camp is scheduled for closure in mid-2017. See http://data.unhcr.org/horn-of-africa/region.php?id=3.

Introduction

1 This history is examined in greater detail in Fraenkel (1964) and Liebenow (1987).

2 The term *civilized* was, and to some degree remains, a widely employed if ill-defined local designation in Liberia. It refers, as Fraenkel put it in the late 1950s, to Liberians considered to be well educated, but even more importantly to those who adopted "Western dress . . . house type and furniture" (1964: 68; see also Moran 1990, 2006: 74–100).

3 There is no easy way to disaggregate the various groups of actors in the story of Monrovia's wartime and postwar urbanization. There is, therefore, no precise way to know how many of the young men who make up Monrovia's male underclass are ex-combatants. Those statistics that do exist, however, paint a staggering picture. The United Nations' final report on the Disarmament, Demobilisation, Rehabilitation and Reintegration Programme (DDRRP), for example, claims that the program enrolled nearly 104,000 ex-fighters. The first disarmament at Camp Schieffelin, a military base just outside the capital, registered almost 13,000 people, and was followed by a number of other disarmament exercises in the Monrovia area. In other words, a significant percentage of those who disarmed after the war did so in the capital and its immediate surroundings, and there is every reason to believe that a good many more ex-combatants made their way to Monrovia

in the war's aftermath. There is no doubt that a significant population of men who bore arms during the war now reside in the city.

4 The UN's final report on the DDRRP was available as of March 16, 2014, at https://erc.undp.org/evaluation/documents/download/1289.

5 See, for example, http://www.globalsecurity.org/military/world/liberia/economy.htm [accessed 19 November 2016]; Teage (2015); Yangian (2013).

6 While there are valid reasons to question whether "ex-combatant" remains a useful demographic denominator a decade after the end of the war (see Käihkö 2015, 2016), my own interest has long been in understanding how the young men caught up in this conflict constituted a labor pool for a particular order of global capitalism. It is, therefore, not so much their historical association with any of the various fighting factions that is relevant here, but their continued subjection to global processes that buffet them at every turn and structure their experience of the city just as it did during the war.

7 For more on the French and Italian colonies of Mediterranean North Africa, see Fuller (2007), Wright (1991), and the essays collected in Avermaete, Karakayali, and von Osten (2010).

8 This is not to say that such efforts are nonexistent. The historian Nnamdi Elleh's (2002) *Architecture and Power* provides one compelling example, analyzing in depth the Basilique Notre-Dame de la Paix in Yamoussoukro (Côte d'Ivoire) and the Grande Mosquée Hassan II in Casablanca (Morocco) as material manifestations of a particular kind of sovereign authority in Africa. A generation earlier, Udo Kultermann (1969) used individual building projects as an entry point for addressing the opportunities and challenges that cities provided newly independent African states for crafting distinct national identities. In postapartheid South Africa, architecture has played an important role in the symbolic crafting of the "rainbow nation," and architects, historians, and theorists have produced a rich body of analysis and critique that looks at both the past and emergent built environment as formal designs and as political forms (Bremner 2004; Judin and Vladislavić 1998; Murray 2008, 2011; Noble 2011). Across the rest of the continent, the 2013 *Afritecture* exhibition and catalog; the ArchiAfrika network's various online and print publications; the anthologies of African writing, theory, and art edited by Edgar Pieterse; and works like Folkers's (2010) *Modern Architecture in Africa* all read new African built forms as serious architecture. Each is an effort to make African forms part of a larger conversation about the role and meaning of the built environment, to understand what might be uniquely local about these forms and how they fit into the global conversation about cities and how we build and inhabit them.

9 Among many analyses of the importance of photography to modern architecture, see for example, Forty (2012), Mostafavi and Leatherbarrow (1993: 111–112), Murphy (2012), Pye (1978: 66), and Zimmerman (2004, 2012).

10 See also Jane Rendell's (2010) useful, though considerably more challenging, *Site-*

Writing, which sets out to create a tripartite relation between written critique, art object, and the architectural space in which art is encountered.

1. Live Dangerously, My Brothers

1 I have written more extensively about Small Dennis and the Guthrie Plantation in Hoffman (2011b).

2 For Deleuze, the society of control was the successor to Michel Foucault's disciplinary society, in which specific kinds of spaces (the clinic, the asylum, the prison, the school, or military barracks) created subjects with a discrete identity. In the society of control, power operates not by creating specific identities for its subjects but by keeping track of where they are located in space.

3 For more on this, see Hoffman (2016).

4 Here I use *worlding* in the sense that Simone (2001) has used it to describe an African urbanism that conceives of the city as a platform from which to leave for other spaces in which opportunities can be found.

5 Peter Johnson's website Heterotopian Studies (http://www.heterotopiastudies .com/) provides a useful resource for understanding Foucault's use of the term and the ways it has influenced other scholars.

6 Chatterjee (2004: 7) himself notes the importance of Foucault's heterotopias to his thinking. To become "political society," a population group requires a physical space in which to be located and through which to define itself. His examples are primarily the squatters in various Calcutta buildings and infrastructures, including abandoned railway stations and college campuses. One of the few things these otherwise heterogenous populations have in common, and around which they build their political claims, is a shared sense of belonging to an urban space and hence, by extension, a community.

7 "Heterotopias of crisis," for example, include those "sacred or forbidden places reserved to individuals who are in a state of crisis in relation to the society in which they live" (Foucault 1986: 24, cited in Shane 2005: 234). The occupants of heterotopias of crisis disappear into enclaves within and between the structures of the city, more or less masked as they experiment with new urban formations.

8 Sometimes consisting of actual built forms, transgressive architectures are more often social and political practices of space that occur outside the purview of authorities because they happen within sites presumed to be dead. Doron's description of the industrial ruin, the quintessential modern dead zone, nicely summarizes his argument: "The industrial ruin is an indeterminate and volatile place: structurally, since it is dilapidating, and socially because, in contrast to formal public space, where the rules of behaviour are determined by norms and laws (often place-bound by-laws), the industrial ruin's space has no such laws. It is agonistic and radically democratic since the ways of being in this place are negotiated between the various groups and individuals who use it rather than those who pass laws elsewhere" (2000).

9 In this sense, Monrovia is strangely in keeping with the way Rem Koolhaas (1978) once described modern New York City: a massive grid in which the different architectural forms of the individual blocks do nothing to arrest the overall flows of the city. In fact, the more diverse and varied the individual forms of the city, the simpler it is for the hegemonic logic of the whole to function without impediment.

2. The Ministry of Defense

1 The two most famous modernist planned cities in the Global South—Brasília, Brazil, and Chandigarh, India—have both been called exemplars of brutalist architecture. In both cases this has more to do with their monumental scale, abstractness, and concrete construction than with direct influence from the Smithsons or their emerging philosophy of new brutalism, though the Smithsons' friends and intellectual partners Maxwell Fry and Jane Drew would eventually work in Chandigarh. For more on Brasília, see Holston (1989). On Chandigarh, see Evenson (1966) and Prakash (2002).

2 By contrast, Caleb Smith (2008) has argued that in the United States, at least, this has always been the basis of systems of incarceration.

3 See introduction. At the end of that year, it was announced that the Chinese government would demolish the ministry and use the land as the site for a massive new ministerial complex, projected to be one of the largest and most expensive constructions in Africa. For the next four years, however, the building stood empty. Then, at last, at the end of October 2016, a Chinese wrecking crew demolished the ministry over several days.

4 The series of books by Jean-Paul Bourdier and Trinh T. Minh-ha (1996, 2011) are among the more intriguing and sophisticated on this question.

3. E. J. Roye

1 The film, apparently from the Tolbert family archives, has been restored by Yor-El Francis of Pepperbird Studios, https://www.youtube.com/watch?v=Jhxoe8MI2U8.

2 The historical record includes differing accounts of Roye's death. Most say he was either executed after being beaten and paraded through the streets, or drowned while trying to escape prison.

3 See, for example, the Richards biography page of the website TLC Africa (The Liberian Connection): "Monrovia, Liberia: E. J. Roye Building," TLC Africa, http://www.tlcafrica.com/pictures/tlcalbum_ejroye.htm.

4 The E. J. Roye seemed in this sense to stand as testament to Paul Virilio's (1977, 1994) argument that the evolution of the city form is propelled by changes in the nature of warfare and the demands of military defense.

5 The Sinkor building boom has been nicely documented and analyzed by Matt Jones in his blog Moved2Monrovia, http://movedtomonrovia.blogspot.com /2013/09/that-sinkor-feeling-two-monrovias.html.

4. Hotel Africa

1 This is something I have explored further in Hoffman (2011a), as well as with Mariane Ferme (Ferme and Hoffman 2004).

2 See also Pelkmans (2003) and Rao (2007) for similar conclusions in different geographic contexts. Victor Buchli (2013, chapter 7) provides a useful summary of much of the literature on ruins in anthropology.

3 I have explored this idea of media-driven spectacles of violence further in relation to the wars in Sierra Leone and Liberia (Hoffman 2004, 2011b).

5. Liberia Broadcasting System

1 Victor Lacken, a Red Cross photographer, accompanied burial teams to the LBS building in 2014 during the Ebola virus disease outbreak. By his estimates there were still 250 people living in the building at the time. See http://www.aid-expo .com/vote-photojournalism-finalists-2015?id=181. The title of this section is borrowed from Charles Piot's (2010) ethnography of the same name.

2 Among the better-known Deleuzian architects are Greg Lynn (1998) and Bernard Cache (1995), both of whom have written about their approach to architecture. See also the useful summary of architects' engagement with Deleuze in Ballantyne (2007).

3 For insightful analyses of just how these various considerations have played out in projects in South Africa, see Bremner (2004) and Noble (2011). As Lepik notes, two recent efforts to create an archive of notable works in Africa are Folkers (2010) and the ArchiAfrika website and magazine (http://archiafrika.org /magazine/).

4 Not having been a part of the European colonial empires in Africa, Liberia's colonial history is obviously somewhat different from that of most of the continent. That said, its relations with the United States until the end of the Cold War are remarkably similar to those of other African states with their former colonial metropoles.

5 For more on the history of factory design and the relationship between factory architecture and production methods, see Biggs (1995).

6 Of particular importance in modern movement architectural discourse, the *parti* or *parti pris* of a structure is the principal concept or idea that animates the entire design.

7 The Larkin Building was demolished in 1950.

6. Finding Urban Form

1 On the characterization of quarantine as an outdated practice, see for example Manaugh (2014) and Manaugh and Twilley (2014). Among the many studies of colonial health policy and the spatial separation of populations around the African continent, see Comaroff and Comaroff (1991), Curtain (1992), Gandy (2014), Hunt (1999), Lagae (2012), Vaughn (1991), and Swanson (1977).

2 Catherine Bolten, comments at the American Anthropological Association Task Force on Ebola conference, November 6–7, 2014.Washington, DC.

3 I should note here that I think many factors were at work in the attack on the West Point Ebola treatment center, including some very powerful narratives about the realities of how Ebola is transmitted, how it could be cured, and who was responsible for it. But in a sense all of these could be considered part of a logic of response that Slavoj Žižek (1997: 28) has called the "empty gesture"—the seemingly irrational choice that makes vividly clear that the gesturer in fact has no choice at all.

References

Abani, Chris. 2005. *Graceland*. New York: Farrar, Straus, and Giroux.

Abdullah, Ibrahim. 1998. "Bush Paths to Destruction: The Origin and Character of the Revolutionary United Front / Sierra Leone." *Journal of Modern African Studies* 36 (2): 203–235.

Abrahamson, Michael. 2011. "Brutalism: The Word Itself and What We Mean When We Say It" [blog post]. *Critic under the Influence*, November 20. https://criticundertheinfluence.wordpress.com.

Adamson, Paul, Marty Arbunich, and Ernie Braun. 2002. *Eichler: Modernism Rebuilds the American Dream*. Salt Lake City, UT: Gibbs Smith.

Adjaye, David. 2011. *African Metropolitan Architecture*. New York: Rizzoli.

Agamben, Giorgio. 1998. *Homo Sacer: Sovereign Power and Bare Life*. Stanford, CA: Stanford University Press.

Agier, Michel. 2002. "Between War and the City: Toward an Urban Anthropology of Refugee Camps." *Ethnography* 3 (3): 317–341.

Agier, Michel. 2008. *On the Margins of the World*. Malden, MA: Polity.

Allweil, Yael, and Rachel Kallus. 2008. "Public-Space Heterotopias: Heterotopias of Masculinity along the Tel Aviv Shoreline." In *Heterotopia and the City: Public Space in a Postcivil Society*, edited by Michiel Dehaene and Lieven De Cauter, 191–202. New York: Routledge.

Anderson, Benedict. 1991. *Imagined Communities: Reflections on the Origins and Spread of Nationalism*. New York: Verso.

Anderson, Jon Lee. 2013. "Slumlord." *New Yorker*, January 28, http://www.newyorker.com/.

Appadurai, Arjun. 1988. *The Social Life of Things: Commodities in Cultural Perspective*. London: Cambridge University Press.

Artweek.LA. 2013. "Iwan Baan: The Way We Live." Exhibition preview. February 18. http://artweek.la/issue/february-18-2013/article/iwan-baan-the-way-we-live.

Aureli, Pier Vittorio. 2011. *The Possibility of an Absolute Architecture*. Cambridge, MA: MIT Press.

Avermaete, Tom, Serhat Karakayali, and Marion von Osten. 2010. *Colonial Modern: Aesthetics of the Past—Rebellions for the Future*. London: Black Dog.

Ballantyne, Andrew. 2007. *Deleuze and Guattari for Architects*. New York: Routledge.

Banham, Reyner. (1955) 2011. "The New Brutalism." *October* 136: 19–28.

Banham, Reyner. 1966. *The New Brutalism: Ethic or Aesthetic?* New York: Reinhold.

Banham, Reyner. 1989. *A Concrete Atlantis: US Industrial Building and European Modern Architecture, 1900–1925*. Cambridge, MA: MIT Press.

Beasley-Murray, Jon. 2010. "Vilcashuamán: Telling Stories in Ruins." In *Ruins of Modernity*, edited by Julia Hell and Andreas Schönle, 212–231. Durham, NC: Duke University Press.

Behrend, Heike. 2013. *Contesting Visibility: Photographic Practices on the East African Coast*. Bielefeld: Transcript.

Benjamin, Walter. 1968. "The Work of Art in the Age of Mechanical Reproduction." In *Illuminations*, 217–253. New York: Harcourt Brace and World.

Benjamin, Walter. 1978a. "Naples." In *Reflections: Essays, Aphorisms, Autobiographical Writings*, 163–173. New York: Harcourt Brace Jovanovich.

Benjamin, Walter. 1978b. "Paris, Capital of the Nineteenth Century." In *Reflections: Essays, Aphorisms, Autobiographical Writings*, 146–162. New York: Harcourt Brace Jovanovich.

Biggs, Lindy. 1995. "The Engineered Factory." *Technology and Culture* 36 (2): S174–S188.

Bond, Patrick. 2006. *Looting Africa: The Economics of Exploitation*. New York: Zed.

Bourdier, Jean-Paul, and Trinh T. Minh-ha. 1996. *Drawn from African Dwellings*. Bloomington: Indiana University Press.

Bourdier, Jean-Paul, and Trinh T. Minh-ha. 2011. *Vernacular Architecture of West Africa: A World in Dwelling*. New York: Routledge.

Brabazon, James, and Jonathan Stack. 2008. *Liberia: An Uncivil War*. New York: Gabriel Films. DVD.

Braziel, Jana Evans. n.d. "Notes on 'What Is a Minor Literature' from *Kafka: Towards a Minor Literature*." http://www.umass.edu/complit/aclanet/janadele.htm.

Bremner, Lindsay. 2004. "Reframing Township Space: The Kliptown Project." *Public Culture* 16 (3): 521–531.

Brown, William J. 1993. "Walter Gropius and Grain Elevators: Misreading Photographs." *History of Photography* 17 (3): 304–308.

Buchanan, Ian, and Greg Lambert. 2005. *Deleuze and Space*. Edinburgh: Edinburgh University Press.

Buchli, Victor. 2013. *An Anthropology of Architecture*. New York: Bloomsbury.

Buck-Morss, Susan. 1986. "The Flâneur, the Sandwich Man, and the Whore: The Politics of Loitering." *New German Critique* 39: 99–140.

Buck-Morss, Susan. 2000. *Dreamworld and Catastrophe: The Passing of Mass Utopia in East and West.* Cambridge, MA: MIT Press.

Buck-Morss, Susan. 2013. "The City as Dreamworld and Catastrophe." *Texts.* http://susanbuckmorss.info.

Burke, Timothy. 1996. *Lifebuoy Men, Lux Women: Commodification, Consumption, and Cleanliness in Modern Zimbabwe.* Durham, NC: Duke University Press.

Butler, Judith. 2004. *Precarious Life: The Powers of Mourning and Violence.* New York: Verso.

Cache, Bernard. 1995. *Earth Moves: The Furnishing of Territories.* Cambridge, MA: MIT Press.

Cairns, Stephen, and Jane M. Jacobs. 2014. *Buildings Must Die: A Perverse View of Architecture.* Cambridge, MA: MIT Press.

Chalfin, Brenda. 2014. "Public Things, Excremental Politics, and the Infrastructure of Bare Life in Ghana's City of Tema." *American Ethnologist* 41 (1): 92–109.

Chan, Kelly. 2012. "Learning from Lagos: Contemporary Architects Harvest the Slums for Design Inspiration." BlouinArtinfo International, June 7, www.blouinartinfo.com/news/story/807260/learning-from-lagos-contemporary-architects-harvest-the-slums.

Chatterjee, Partha. 2004. *The Politics of the Governed: Reflections on Popular Politics in Most of the World.* New York: Columbia University Press.

Cho, Mun Young. 2013. *The Specter of "the People": Urban Poverty in Northeast China.* Ithaca, NY: Cornell University Press.

Christensen, Maya. 2013. "Shadow Soldiering: Mobilisation, Militarisation and the Politics of Global Security in Sierra Leone." PhD diss., Institut for Antropologi, Copenhagen University.

Christensen, Maya, and Mats Utas. 2008. "Mercenaries of Democracy: The 'Politricks' of Remobilized Combatants in the 2007 General Elections, Sierra Leone." *African Affairs* 107 (429): 515–539.

Clapham, Christopher. 1976. *Liberia and Sierra Leone: An Essay in Comparative Politics.* New York: Cambridge University Press.

Cohen, Abner. 1969. *Custom and Politics in Urban Africa.* London: Routledge.

Cohen, Abner. 1981. *The Politics of Elite Culture: Explorations in the Dramaturgy of Power in a Modern African Society.* Berkeley: University of California Press.

Cohen, Jean-Louis. 1999. "Le Corbusier's Nietzschean Metaphors." In *Nietzsche and "An Architecture of Our Minds,"* edited by Alexandre Kostka and Irving Wohlfarth, 311–332. Los Angeles: Getty Research Institute.

Cohen, Jean-Louis. 2011. *Architecture in Uniform: Designing and Building for the Second World War.* Montreal: Canadian Centre for Architecture.

Cohen, Jean-Louis. 2012. *The Future of Architecture since 1889.* New York: Phaidon.

Comaroff, Jean, and John L. Comaroff. 1991. *Of Revelation and Revolution: Volume 1—Christianity, Colonialism, and Consciousness in South Africa.* Chicago: University of Chicago Press.

Coward, Martin. 2009. *Urbicide: The Politics of Urban Destruction.* New York: Routledge.

Crinson, Mark. 2003. *Modern Architecture and the End of Empire.* Aldershot, U.K.: Ashgate.

Crosby, Theo. (1955) 2011. "The New Brutalism." *October* 136: 17–18.

Curtain, Philip D. 1992. "Medical Knowledge and Urban Planning in Colonial Tropical Africa." In *The Social Basis of Health and Healing in Africa*, edited by Steven Feierman and John M. Janzen, 235–255. Berkeley: University of California Press.

Curtis, William. 1996. *Modern Architecture since 1900.* New York: Phaidon.

Dago, Ananias Leki, and Yann Le Goff. 2003. *Ananias Leki Dago: Photographe.* Montreuil: Editions de l'oeil.

D'Alisera, JoAnn. 2004. *Imagined Geography: Sierra Leonean Muslims in America.* Philadelphia: University of Pennsylvania Press.

Darley, Gillian. 2003. *Factory.* London: Reaktion.

de Boeck, Filip. 2011. "Inhabiting Ocular Ground: Kinshasa's Future in the Light of Congo's Spectral Urban Politics." *Cultural Anthropology* 26 (2): 263–286.

de Boeck, Filip. 2013. "Challenges of Urban Growth: Toward an Anthropology of Urban Infrastructure." In *Afritecture: Building Social Change*, edited by Andres Lepik, 92–103. Ostfildern: Hatje Cantz.

de Boeck, Filip, and Marie-Françoise Plissart. 2005. *Kinshasa: Tales of the Invisible City.* Ghent: Ludion.

Deleuze, Gilles. 1989. *The Time-Image: Cinema 2.* Minneapolis: University of Minnesota Press.

Deleuze, Gilles. 1992. *The Fold: Leibniz and the Baroque.* Minneapolis: University of Minnesota Press.

Deleuze, Gilles. 1995. *Negotiations: 1972–1990.* Translated by Martin Joughin. Edited by Lawrence Kritzman. European Perspectives. New York: Columbia University Press.

Deleuze, Gilles, and Félix Guattari. 1983. *Anti-Oedipus: Capitalism and Schizophrenia*, vol. 1. Minneapolis: University of Minnesota Press.

Deleuze, Gilles, and Félix Guattari. 1986. *Kafka: Toward a Minor Literature.* Minneapolis: University of Minnesota Press.

Deleuze, Gilles, and Félix Guattari. 1987. *A Thousand Plateaus: Capitalism and Schizophrenia*, vol. 2. Minneapolis: University of Minnesota Press.

de Maat, Sytse. 2009. "Slum, the Vernacular Architecture of Swelling Cities." *Perfect Slum*, November. http://theperfectslum.blogspot.fr/2009/11/slum.html.

Denison, Edward, Yu Ren Guang, and Naigzy Gebremedhin. 2007. *Asmara: Africa's Secret Modernist City.* New York: Merrell.

Desjarlais, Robert. 2015. "Seared with Reality: Phenomenology through Photography, in Nepal." In *Phenomenology in Anthropology: A Sense of Perspective*, edited by Kalpana Ram and Christopher Houston, 197-223. Bloomington: Indiana University Press.

de Wet, Chris, ed. 2006. *Development-Induced Displacement: Problems, Policies and People*. New York: Berghan.

Doron, Gil. 2000. "The Dead Zone and the Architecture of Transgression." *City* 4 (2): 247–263.

Doron, Gil. 2007. ". . . Badlands, Black Space, Border Vacuums, Brown Fields, Conceptual Nevada, Dead Zones." *Field* 1 (1): 10–23.

Edensor, Tim. 2005a. *Industrial Ruins: Spaces, Aesthetics and Materiality*. New York: Berg.

Edensor, Tim. 2005b. "Waste Matter—the Debris of Industrial Ruins and the Disordering of the Material World." *Journal of Material Culture* 10 (3): 311–332.

Elleh, Nnamdi. 1997. *African Architecture: Evolution and Transformation*. New York: McGraw-Hill.

Elleh, Nnamdi. 2002. *Architecture and Power in Africa*. Westport, CT: Praeger.

Ellis, Stephen. 1999. *The Mask of Anarchy: The Destruction of Liberia and the Religious Dimensions of an African Civil War*. New York: New York University Press.

Enwezor, Okwui. 2006. *Snap Judgments: New Positions in Contemporary African Photography*. New York: International Center of Photography and Steidl.

Enwezor, Okwui. 2007. "The Indeterminate Structure of Things Now: Notes on Contemporary South African Photography." *Bedeutung* 1. http://www.bedeutung .co.uk/magazine/issues/1-nature-culture/enwezor-indeterminate-structure/.

Enwezor, Okwui. 2010. "Modernity and Postcolonial Ambivalence." *South Atlantic Quarterly* 109 (3): 595–620.

Evenson, Norma. 1966. *Chandigarh*. Berkeley: University of California Press.

Ferguson, James. 1990. *The Anti-politics Machine: "Development," Depoliticization, and Bureaucratic Power in Lesotho*. Cambridge, MA: Harvard University Press.

Ferguson, James. 1999. *Expectations of Modernity: Myths and Meanings of Urban Life on the Zambian Copperbelt*. Berkeley: University of California Press.

Ferguson, James. 2006. *Global Shadows: Africa in the Neoliberal World Order*. Durham, NC: Duke University Press.

Ferme, Mariane, and Danny Hoffman. 2004. "Hunter Militias and the New Human Rights Discourse in Sierra Leone and Beyond." *Africa Today* 50 (4): 73–95.

Folkers, Antoni. 2010. *Modern Architecture in Africa*. Amsterdam: Sun.

Forty, Adrian. 2012. *Concrete and Culture: A Material History*. London: Reaktion.

Foucault, Michel. 1978. "About the Concept of the 'Dangerous Individual' in 19th Century Legal Psychiatry." *International Journal of Law and Psychiatry* 1: 1–18.

Foucault, Michel. 1986. "Of Other Spaces." *Diacritics* 16 (spring): 22–27.

Fraenkel, Merran. 1964. *Tribe and Class in Monrovia*. London: Oxford University Press.

Frampton, Kenneth. 1990. "Rappel à l'ordre: The Case for the Tectonic." *Architectural Design* 60 (3–4): 19–25.

Frascari, Marco. 1984. "The Tell Tale Detail." *VIA 7: The Building of Architecture*: 23–37.

Frenkel, Stephen, and John Western. 1988. "Pretext or Prophylaxis? Racial Segregation and Malarial Mosquitos in a British Tropical Colony: Sierra Leone." *Annals of the Association of American Geographers* 78 (2): 211–228.

Fry, Maxwell, and Jane Drew. 1956. *Tropical Architecture in the Humid Zone.* New York: Reinhold.

Fuller, Mia. 2007. *Moderns Abroad: Architecture, Cities, and Italian Imperialism.* New York: Routledge.

Gandy, Matthew. 2014. *The Fabric of Space: Water, Modernity, and the Urban Imagination.* Cambridge, MA: MIT Press.

Gberie, Lansana. 2005. *A Dirty War in West Africa: The RUF and the Destruction of Sierra Leone.* Bloomington: Indiana University Press.

Geertz, Clifford. 1973. *The Interpretation of Cultures: Selected Essays.* New York: Basic Books.

Gluckman, Max. 1960. "Tribalism in Modern British Central Africa." *Cahiers d'études africaines* 1 (1): 55–70.

Gogan, Nicky, and Paul Rowley. 2011. *Build Something Modern.* Dublin: Still Films. DVD.

Gold, John R. 1997. *The Experience of Modernism: Modern Architects and the Future City, 1928–1953.* New York: E. and F. N. Spon.

Gordillo, Gastón. 2011. "Ships Stranded in the Forest: Debris of Progress on a Phantom River." *Current Anthropology* 52 (2): 141–167.

Gordillo, Gastón. 2014. *Rubble: The Afterlife of Destruction.* Durham, NC: Duke University Press.

Grosz, Elizabeth. 2001. *Architecture from the Outside: Essays on Virtual and Real Space.* Cambridge, MA: MIT Press.

Guidi, Guido. 2011. *Carlo Scarpa: Brion.* Ostfildern: Hatje Cantz.

Häntzschel, Jörg. 2013. "At Home in the World: Iwan Baan, Documentalist of Constructed and Inhabited Space." In Iwan Baan, *52 Weeks, 52 Cities*, 6–8. Berlin: Kehrer.

Hardt, Michael. 1995. "The Withering of Civil Society." *Social Text* 14, no. 4: 27–44.

Harvey, David. 2000. *Spaces of Hope.* Edinburgh: Edinburgh University Press.

Harvey, David. 2012. *Rebel Cities: From the Right to the City to the Urban Revolution.* New York: Verso.

Havesit, Dennis. 2012. "Gerhard Kallman, Architect, Dies at 97." *New York Times,* June 25, A13.

Heidegger, Martin. 1993. *Basic Writings.* New York: HarperCollins.

Hell, Julia, and Andreas Schönle, eds. 2010. *Ruins of Modernity.* Durham, NC: Duke University Press.

Hepner, Tricia Redeker. 2009. *Soldiers, Martyrs, Traitors and Exiles: Political Conflict in Eritrea and the Diaspora.* Philadelphia: University of Pennsylvania Press.

Herscher, Andrew. 2010a. "Cover Interview: Andrew Herscher." *Rorotoko,* August 2. http://rorotoko.com/interview/20100802_herscher_andrew_violence_taking _place_architecture_kosovo_conflict/.

Herscher, Andrew. 2010b. *Violence Taking Place: The Architecture of the Kosovo Conflict.* Stanford, CA: Stanford University Press.

Hess, Janet Berry. 2000. "Imagining Architecture: The Structure of Nationalism in Accra, Ghana." *Africa Today* 47 (2): 35–58.

Hess, Janet Berry. 2006. *Art and Architecture in Postcolonial Africa.* Jefferson, NC: McFarland.

Hetherington, Tim. 2009. *Long Story Bit by Bit: Liberia Retold.* New York: Umbrage.

Hoffman, Danny. 2004. "The Civilian Target in Sierra Leone and Liberia: Political Power, Military Strategy, and Humanitarian Intervention." *African Affairs* 103 (411): 211–226.

Hoffman, Danny. 2006. "Despot Deposed: Charles Taylor and the Challenge of State Reconstruction in Liberia." In *Legacies of Power: Leadership Change and Former Presidents in African Politics*, edited by Roger Southall and Henning Melber, 308–331. Pretoria: HSRC Press.

Hoffman, Danny. 2011a. "Violence, Just in Time: War and Work in Contemporary West Africa." *Cultural Anthropology* 26 (1): 34–57.

Hoffman, Danny. 2011b. *The War Machines: Young Men and Violence in Sierra Leone and Liberia.* Durham, NC: Duke University Press.

Hoffman, Danny. 2016. "Brokering Revolution: Imagining Revolution on the West African Borderlands." In *African Futures: Essays on Crisis, Emergence, and Possibility*, edited by Brian Goldstone and Juan Obarrio, 95–103. Chicago: University of Chicago Press.

Holston, James. 1989. *The Modernist City: An Anthropological Critique of Brasília.* Chicago: University of Chicago Press.

Holston, James. 2008. *Insurgent Citizenship: Disjunctions of Democracy and Modernity in Brazil.* Princeton, NJ: Princeton University Press.

Hou, Jeffrey, ed. 2010. *Insurgent Public Space: Guerrilla Urbanism and the Remaking of Contemporary Cities.* New York: Routledge.

Huband, Mark. 1998. *The Liberian Civil War.* Portland, OR: F. Cass.

Hughes, Ailey Kaiser. 2013. "Using Land Policy to Improve Life for the Urban Poor: Liberia." Briefing paper, Focus on Land in Africa.

Hunt, Nancy Rose. 1999. *A Colonial Lexicon: Of Birth Ritual, Medicalization, and Mobility in the Congo.* Durham, NC: Duke University Press.

Ingold, Tim. 2013. *Making: Anthropology, Archaeology, Art and Architecture.* New York: Routledge.

Jackson, Michael. 2012. *Lifeworlds: Essays in Existential Anthropology.* Chicago: University of Chicago Press.

Jameson, Fredric. 1991. *Postmodernism, or, the Cultural Logic of Late Capitalism.* Durham, NC: Duke University Press.

Judin, Hilton, and Ivan Vladislavić. 1998. *Blank: Architecture, Apartheid and After.* Rotterdam: NAi.

Juris, Jeff. 2012. "Reflecting on #Occupy Everywhere: Social Media, Public Space, and Emerging Logics of Aggregation." *American Ethnologist* 39 (2): 259–279.

Juris, Jeff, and Maple Razsa. 2012. "Occupy, Anthropology, and the 2011 Global Uprisings." *Cultural Anthropology*, July 27. https://culanth.org/fieldsights/63 -occupy-anthropology-and-the-2011-global-uprisings.

Käihkö, Ilmari. 2015. "'No Die, No Rest'? Coercive Discipline in Liberian Military Organisations." *Africa Spectrum* 50 (2): 3–29.

Käihkö, Ilmari. 2016. "Bush Generals and Small Boy Battalions: Military Cohesion in Liberia and Beyond." PhD diss., Uppsala University, Sweden.

Karmo, Henry. 2012. "Complex Solution: Site for New Ministerial Facility in Liberia Not Shy of Controversy." *Front Page Africa* 21 (3): 1–3.

Kasco, Dorris Haron, and Jean Christophe Deberre. 1994. *Dorris Haron Kasco: Les Fous D'Abidjan.* Paris: Revue Noire.

Kaufmann, Andrea. 2016. "Spaces of Imagination: Associational Life and the State in Post-War, Urban Liberia." PhD diss., University of Basel, Switzerland.

Kitnick, Alex. 2011. "Introduction." *October* 136: 3–6.

Klein, Naomi. 2007. *The Shock Doctrine: The Rise of Disaster Capitalism.* New York: Metropolitan.

Koolhaas, Rem. 1978. *Delirious New York: A Retroactive Manifesto for Manhattan.* New York: Oxford University Press.

Koolhaas, Rem. 2002. "Fragments of a Lecture on Lagos." In *Under Siege: Four African Cities—Freetown, Johannesburg, Kinshasa, Lagos.* Documenta 11, Platform 4, edited by Okwui Enwezor et al., 173–183. Ostfildern-Ruit: Hatje Cantz.

Kultermann, Udo. 1963. *New Architecture in Africa.* New York: Universe.

Kultermann, Udo. 1969. *New Directions in African Architecture.* New York: G. Brazilier.

La Cecla, Franco. 2012. *Against Architecture.* Oakland, CA: PM Press.

Lagae, Johan. 2012. "Towards a Rough Guide for Lubumbashi." In *African Perspectives [South Africa]: City, Society, Space, Literature, and Architecture,* edited by Gerhard Bruyns. Rotterdam: 010 Publishers.

Lamuniere, Michelle. 2001. *You Look Beautiful Like That: The Portrait Photographs of Seydou Keïta and Malick Sidibé.* Cambridge, MA: Harvard University Art Museums.

Larkin, Brian. 2008. *Signal and Noise: Media, Infrastructure and Urban Culture in Nigeria.* Durham, NC: Duke University Press.

Leatherbarrow, David, and Moshen Mostafavi. 2002. *Surface Architecture.* Cambridge, MA: MIT Press.

Le Corbusier. 2007. *Toward an Architecture.* Los Angeles: Getty Research Institute.

Lefebvre, Henri. 2003. *The Urban Revolution.* Minneapolis: University of Minnesota Press.

Lelong, M.-H. 1946. *L'Afrique noire sans les blancs.* Alger: Baconnier.

Lepik, Andres, ed. 2013. *Afritecture: Building Social Change.* Ostfildern: Hatje Cantz.

le Roux, Hannah. 2003. "The Networks of Tropical Architecture." *Journal of Architecture* 8 (3): 337–354.

le Roux, Hannah, and Ola Uduku. 2004. "The Media and the Modern Movement in Nigeria and the Gold Coast." *Nka: Journal of Contemporary African Art* 19 (summer): 46–49.

Leslie, Esther. 2006. "Ruin and Rubble in the Arcades." In *Walter Benjamin and the Arcades Project, edited by Beatrice* Hanssen, 87–112. London: Continuum.

Levine, Caroline. 2015. *Forms: Whole, Rhythm, Hierarchy, Network.* Princeton, NJ: Princeton University Press.

"Liberia: GoL Sued over Plan to Demolish New Defense Ministry." 2012. *Heritage,* October 2. AllAfrica, http://allafrica.com/stories/201210020855.html.

"Liberia: TWP Partisans Want Gov't Stay Away from Party's Building." 2013. *Inquirer* (Monrovia), November 22. AllAfrica, http://allafrica.com/stories/201311221588 .html?viewall=1.

Liebenow, Gus. 1987. *Liberia: The Quest for Democracy.* Bloomington: Indiana University Press.

Liscombe, Rhodri Windsor. 2006. "Modernism in Late Imperial British West Africa." *Journal of the Society of Architectural Historians* 65 (2): 188–215.

Little, Kenneth. 1965. *West African Urbanization: A Study of Voluntary Associations in Social Change.* Cambridge: Cambridge University Press.

Little, Kenneth. 1974. *Urbanization as a Social Process: An Essay on Movement and Change in Contemporary Africa.* Boston: Routledge and Paul.

Lupick, Travis. 2012a. "Demolitions Ravage Liberia Neighborhoods." *Al Jazeera,* August 12. http://www.aljazeera.com/indepth/features/2012/08/20128271954727559 .html.

Lupick, Travis. 2012b. "Uprooting Liberia: Monrovia's Slum Clearances." ThinkAfricaPress, April 11. http://www.tlupick.com/uprooting-liberia-clearing -monrovias-slums/.

Lynn, Greg. 1998. *Folds, Bodies and Blobs: Collected Essays.* Brussels: La Lettre Volée.

MacGaffey, Janet, and Rémy Bazenguissa-Ganga. 2000. *Congo-Paris: Transnational Traders on the Margin of the Law.* Bloomington: Indiana University Press.

Maher, Stephanie. 2015. "Barça ou Barzakh: The Social Elsewhere of Failed Clandestine Migration out of Senegal." PhD diss., University of Washington.

Manaugh, Geoff. 2014. "The Powers of Quarantine" [blog post]. *BLDGBLOG,* August 21, http://www.bldgblog.com/2014/08/powers-of-quarantine/.

Manaugh, Geoff, and Nicola Twilley. 2014. "Ebola and the Fiction of Quarantine." *New Yorker,* August 11.

Marx, Karl. (1867) 1977. *Capital: A Critique of Political Economy*, vol. 1. New York: Vintage.

Massey, Jonathan, and Brett Snyder. 2012. "Occupying Wall Street: Places and Spaces of Political Action." *Places Journal,* September. https://placesjournal.org/article /occupying-wall-street-places-and-spaces-of-political-action/.

Matt, Gerald, and Thomas Mießgang. 2001. *¡Flash Afrique! Photography from West Africa*. Göttingen: Steidl.

Mbembe, Achille. 1992. "The Banality of Power and the Aesthetics of Vulgarity in the Postcolony." *Public Culture* 4 (2): 1–30.

Mbembe, Achille. 2003. "Necropolitics." *Public Culture* 15 (1): 11–40.

Mbembe, Achille. 2006. "On Politics as a Form of Expenditure." In *Law and Disorder in the Postcolony*, edited by Jean Comaroff and John L. Comaroff, 299–335. Chicago: University of Chicago Press.

Mbembe, Achille, and Janet Roitman. 1995. "Figures of the Subject in Times of Crisis." *Public Culture* 7 (2): 323–352.

McDowell, Christopher, ed. 1996. *Understanding Impoverishment: The Consequences of Development-Induced Displacement*. New York: Berghahn.

McDowell, Christopher. 2014. "Bushmeat and the Politics of Disgust." *Cultural Anthropology*, October 7. http://www.culanth.org/fieldsights/588-bushmeat-and -the-politics-of-disgust.

Meyer, Birgitte. 1999. "Popular Ghanaian Cinema and African Heritage." *Africa Today* 46 (2): 93–114.

Mießgang, Thomas. 2001. "Directors, Flaneurs, Bricoleurs." In *¡Flash Afrique! Photography from West Africa*, edited by Gerald Matt and Thomas Mießgang. Göttingen: Steidl.

Mofokeng, Santu. 2012. *Santu Mofokeng: The Black Photo Album / Look at Me, 1890–1950*. Göttingen: Steidl.

Moran, Mary. 1990. *Civilized Women: Gender and Prestige in Southeastern Liberia*. Ithaca, NY: Cornell University Press.

Moran, Mary. 2006. *Liberia: The Violence of Democracy*. Philadelphia: University of Pennsylvania Press.

Mostafavi, Mohsen, and David Leatherbarrow. 1993. *On Weathering: The Life of Buildings in Time*. Cambridge, MA: MIT Press.

Munive, Jairo. 2011. "A Political Economic History of the Liberian State, Forced Labour and Armed Mobilization." *Journal of Agrarian Change* 11 (3): 357–376.

Murphy, Douglas. 2012. *The Architecture of Failure*. Winchester: Zero.

Murray, Martin. 2008. *Taming the Disorderly City: The Spatial Landscape of Johannesburg after Apartheid*. Ithaca, NY: Cornell University Press.

Murray, Martin. 2011. *City of Extremes: The Spatial Politics of Johannesburg*. Durham, NC: Duke University Press.

Myers, Garth. 2003. *Verandahs of Power: Colonialism and Space in Urban Africa*. Syracuse, NY: Syracuse University Press.

Myers, Garth. 2011. *African Cities: Alternative Visions of Urban Theory and Practice*. New York: Zed.

Nading, Alex M. 2014. *Mosquito Trails: Ecology, Health, and the Politics of Entanglements*. Berkeley: University of California Press.

Neuwirth, Robert. 2004. *Shadow Cities: A Billion Squatters, a New Urban World*. New York: Routledge.

Newell, Sasha. 2012. *The Modernity Bluff: Crime, Consumption, and Citizenship in Côte d'Ivoire*. Chicago: University of Chicago Press.

Nietzsche, Friedrich. 1974. *The Gay Science*. New York: Random House.

Nitzan-Shiftan, Alona. 2007. "The Walled City and the White City: The Construction of the Tel Aviv/Jerusalem Dichotomy." *Perspecta* 39: 92–104.

Nitzan-Shiftan, Alona. 2010. "The Israeli 'Place' in East Jerusalem: How Israeli Architects Appropriated the Palestinian Aesthetic." In *Colonial Modern: Aesthetics of the Past—Rebellions for the Future*, edited by Tom Avermaete, Serhat Karakayali, and Marion von Osten, 88–97. London: Black Dog.

Njami, Simon. 2001. "The Spores of the Stamen." In *Africas: The Artist and the City, a Journey and an Exhibition*, edited by Pep Subirós, 72–75. Barcelona: Centre de Cultura Contemporània de Barcelona.

Noble, Jonathan. 2011. *African Identity in Post-apartheid Public Architecture: White Skin, Black Masks*. Burlington, VT: Ashgate.

Norton, Gregory. 2011. "Searching for Soap Trees: Norwegian Refugee Council's Land Dispute Resolution Process in Liberia." Thematic Report from the Norwegian Refugee Council, January.

Nunley, John. 1987. *Moving with the Face of the Devil: Art and Politics in Urban West Africa*. Urbana: University of Illinois Press.

Oguibe, Olu. 2001. "The Photographic Experience: Toward an Understanding of Photography in Africa." In *¡Flash Afrique! Photography from West Africa*, edited by Gerald Matt and Thomas Mießgang. Göttingen: Steidl.

Olga, Lafazani. 2013. "A Border within a Border: The Migrants' Squatter Settlement in Patras as a Heterotopia." *Journal of Borderlands Studies* 28 (1): 1–13.

Olukoju, Ayodeji. 2006. *Culture and Customs of Liberia*. Westport, CT: Greenwood.

Østervang, Charlotte. 2008. *Fristaden: Christiana 2004–2008*. Copenhagen: Verve.

Parley, Winston. 2013. "Liberia: Government Targets Unfinished Defense Ministry." *New Dawn*, November 18. AllAfrica, http://allafrica.com/stories/201311180879.html.

Pelkmans, Mathijs. 2003. "The Social Life of Empty Buildings: Imagining the Transition in Post-Soviet Ajaria." *Focaal* 41: 121–136.

Peterson, Kristin. 2014. *Speculative Markets: Drug Circuits and Derivative Life in Nigeria*. Durham, NC: Duke University Press.

Pieterse, Edgar. 2008. *City Futures: Confronting the Crisis of Urban Development*. London: Zed.

Pieterse, Edgar, and AbdouMaliq Simone. 2013. *Rogue Urbanism: Emergent African Cities*. Auckland Park, RSA: Jacana.

Piot, Charles. 2010. *Nostalgia for the Future: West Africa after the Cold War*. Chicago: University of Chicago Press.

Piot, Charles. 2012. "Migration Stories: The US Visa Lottery and Global Citizenship." Lecture, Department of Anthropology Colloquium series, fall, University of Washington.

Pivin, Jean Loup. 1999. "La terre en pierre." *Revue Noire* 31: 1–7.

Prakash, Vikramaditya. 2002. *Chandigarh's Le Corbusier: The Struggle for Modernity in Postcolonial India*. Seattle: University of Washington Press.

Pye, David. 1978. *The Nature and Art of Workmanship*. Cambridge: Cambridge University Press.

Pype, Katrien. 2007. "Fighting Boys, Strong Men and Gorillas: Notes on the Imagination of Masculinities in Kinshasa." *Africa* 77 (2): 250–277.

Quayson, Ato. 2010. "Signs of the Times: Discourse Ecologies and Street Life." *City and Society* 22 (1): 77–96.

Rabinow, Paul. 1989. *French Modern: Norms and Forms of the Social Environment*. Cambridge, MA: MIT Press.

Rao, Vyjayanthi. 2007. "Venture Capital." *Public Culture* 19 (3): 593–609.

Rashid, Ismail. 2004. "Student Radicals, Lumpen Youth, and the Origins of Revolutionary Groups in Sierra Leone, 1977–1996." In *Between Democracy and Terror: The Sierra Leone Civil War*, edited by Ibrahim Abdullah, 66–89. Dakar: CODESRIA.

Rendell, Jane. 2010. *Site-Writing: The Architecture of Art Criticism*. New York: I.B. Tauris.

Reno, William. 1998. *Warlord Politics and African States*. Boulder, CO: Lynne Rienner.

Rhodes, Lorna. 2004. *Total Confinement: Madness and Region in the Maximum Security Prison*. Berkeley: University of California Press.

Richards, Paul. 1996. *Fighting for the Rainforest: War, Youth and Resources in Sierra Leone*. Portsmouth, NH: Heinemann.

Robinson, Jennifer. 2006. *Ordinary Cities: Between Modernity and Development*. New York: Routledge.

Sawyer, Amos. 2005. *Beyond Plunder: Toward Democratic Governance in Liberia*. Boulder, CO: Lynne Rienner.

Schim van der Loeff, Sanne. 2014. *"Book Review: 52 Weeks, 52 Cities." GUP Magazine, May 1*. http://www.gupmagazine.com/books/iwan-baan/52-weeks-52-cities.

Scott, James. 1998. *Seeing Like a State: How Certain Schemes to Improve the Human Condition Have Failed*. New Haven, CT: Yale University Press.

Shane, David Grahame. 2005. *Recombinant Urbanism: Conceptual Modeling in Architecture, Urban Design, and City Theory*. Chichester: Wiley-Academy.

Shaw, Rosalind. 2007a. "Displacing Violence: Making Pentecostal Memory in Postwar Sierra Leone." *Cultural Anthropology* 22 (1): 65–92.

Shaw, Rosalind. 2007b. "Memory Frictions: Localizing Truth and Reconciliation in Sierra Leone." *International Journal of Transitional Justice* 1: 183–207.

Shulman, Julius. 1997. "The Fear of Architecture: A Photo-Essay." In *The Architecture of Fear*, edited by Nan Ellin, 121–132. New York: Princeton Architectural Press.

Simmel, Georg. 1976. "The Metropolis and Mental Life." In *The Sociology of Georg Simmel*, edited and translated by Kurt H. Wolff. New York: Free Press.

Simone, AbdouMaliq. 2001. "On the Worlding of African Cities." *African Studies Review* 44 (2): 15–42.

Simone, AbdouMaliq. 2002. "The Visible and the Invisible: Remaking Cities in

Africa." In *Under Siege: Four African Cities—Freetown, Johannesburg, Kinshasa, Lagos*, edited by Okwui Enwezor, 23–44. Ostfilden: Hatje-Cantz.

Simone, AbdouMaliq. 2004. *For the City Yet to Come: Changing Life in Four African Cities*. Durham, NC: Duke University Press.

Smith, Caleb. 2008. "Detention without Subjects: Prisons and the Poetics of Living Death." *Texas Studies in Literature and Language* 50 (3): 243–267.

Smith, Maya. 2015. "Multilingual Practices of Senegalese Immigrants in Rome: Construction of Identities and Negotiation of Boundaries." *Italian Culture* 33 (2): 126–146.

Smithson, Alison, and Peter Smithson. (1957) 2011. "The New Brutalism." *October* 136: 37.

Smithson, Peter. 2001. *The Charged Void: Architecture*. New York: Monacelli.

Sniadecki, J. P. 2014. "Chaiqian/Demolition: Reflections on Media Practice." *Visual Anthropology Review* 30 (1): 23–37.

Soja, Edward. 1996. *Thirdspace: Journeys to Los Angeles and Other Real-and-Imagined Places*. New York: Blackwell.

Solnit, Rebecca. 2005. *A Field Guide to Getting Lost*. New York: Viking.

Steiner, Heider. 2006. "Silo Dreams: The Grain Elevator and Modern Architecture." In *Reconsidering Concrete Atlantis: Buffalo Grain Elevators*, edited by Lynda H. Scheenkloth, 102–114. Buffalo, NY: Design Project.

Stoler, Ann Laura. 2008. "Imperial Debris: Reflections on Ruins and Ruination." *Cultural Anthropology* 23 (2): 191–219.

Stoler, Ann Laura. 2013. "'The Rot Remains': From Ruins to Ruination." In *Imperial Debris: On Ruins and Ruination*, edited by Ann Laura Stoler, 1–37. Durham, NC: Duke University Press.

Stoner, Jill. 2012. *Toward a Minor Architecture*. Cambridge, MA: MIT Press.

Sudjic, Deyan. 2011. *The Edifice Complex: The Architecture of Power*. London: Penguin.

Swanson, Maynard. 1977. "The Sanitation Syndrome: Bubonic Plague and Urban Native Policy in the Cape Colony, 1900–1909." *Journal of African History* 13(3): 387–410.

Tafuri, Manfredo. 1976. *Architecture and Utopia: Design and Capitalist Development*. Cambridge, MA: MIT Press.

Taylor, Lucien. 1996. "Iconophobia." *Transition* 69: 64–88.

Teage, Constance. 2015. "Liberia's Youth Unemployment Problem." The Bush Chicken, February 10. http://www.bushchicken.com/liberias-youth -unemployment-problem/.

Tedlock, Dennis. 2013. *An Archaeology of Architecture: Photowriting the Built Environment*. Albuquerque: University of New Mexico Press.

Thomas, Dominic. 2003. "'La Sape' and Vestimentary Codes in Transnational Contexts and Urban Diasporas." *MLN* 118 (4): 947–973.

Thomas, Lynn. 2006. "The Modern Girl and Racial Respectability in 1930s South Africa." *Journal of African History* 47: 461–490.

Tillim, Guy. 2005. *Jo'burg*. Johannesburg: STE.

Tillim, Guy. 2009. *Avenue Patrice Lumumba*. New York: Prestel.

Tormey, Jane. 2013. *Cities and Photography*. New York: Routledge.

Uduku, Olu. 2006. "Modernist Architecture and 'the Tropical' in West Africa: The Tropical Architecture Movement in West Africa, 1948–1970." *Habitat International* 30 (3): 396–411.

Urban Think Tank. 2013. *Torre David: Informal Vertical Communities*. Zurich: Lars Müller.

van door Horn, Mélanie. 2009. *Indispensable Eyesores: An Anthropology of Undesired Buildings*. New York: Berghahn.

Vaughn, Megan. 1991. *Curing Their Ills: Colonial Power and African Illness*. Stanford, CA: Stanford University Press.

Venturi, Robert, Denise Scott-Brown, and Steven Izenour. 1972. *Learning from Las Vegas*. Cambridge, MA: MIT Press.

Virilio, Paul. 1977. *Speed and Politics: An Essay in Dromology*. New York: Semiotext(e).

Virilio, Paul. 1994. *Bunker Archaeology*. Princeton, NJ: Princeton University Press.

Wainaina, Binyavanga. 2005. "Inventing Nairobi." Video interview, National Geographic Society. http://ngm.nationalgeographic.com/2005/09/nairobi/video-wainaina-interactive.

Wallerstein, Even-Olav. 2008. *The Silence of Mies*. Stockholm: Axl Books.

Way, Thaisa. 2013. "Landscapes of Industrial Excess: A Thick Sections Approach to Gas Works Park." *Journal of Landscape Architecture* 8 (1): 28–39.

Weiss, Brad. 2002. "Thug Realism: Inhabiting Fantasy in Urban Tanzania." *Cultural Anthropology* 17 (1): 93–124.

Wendl, Tobias. 2001. "Visions of Modernity in Ghana: Mami Wata Shrines, Photo Studios and Horror Films." *Visual Anthropology* 14 (3): 269–292.

Williams, Rhodri C. 2011. "Beyond's Squatters Rights: Durable Solutions and Development—Induced Displacement in Monrovia, Liberia." Thematic Report #4, Norwegian Refugee Council.

Woods, Lebbeus. 1993. *War and Architecture*. New York: Princeton Architectural Press.

Wright, Gwendolyn. 1991. *The Politics of Design in French Colonial Urbanism*. Chicago: University of Chicago Press.

Yangian, Kennedy L. 2013. "Liberia: Unemployment Rate Falls Far below 85 Percent, Deputy Labour Minister Tells Incoming Boss." AllAfrica, June 21. http://allafrica.com/stories/201306210915.html.

Zimmerman, Claire. 2004. "Photographic Modern Architecture: Inside 'The New Deep.'" *Journal of Architecture* 9: 331–354.

Zimmerman, Claire. 2012. "Photography into Building in Postwar Architecture: The Smithsons and James Stirling." *Art History* 35: 270–287.

Žižek, Slavoj. 1997. *The Plague of Fantasies*. New York: Verso.

Index